PRIMER contents

> "*The gospel is the glorious news that the God who is himself **holy** freely shares that **holiness** in covenant with us and, when we refuse that **holiness** in sin, graciously gives us **holiness** yet again in Christ.*"

Michael Allen, *Sanctification* (Grand Rapids: Zondervan, 2017), 34.

I'm not sure I've ever heard the gospel preached that way, and I wonder what you make of it. Count them: no less than four uses of the words holy/holiness.

Now you might wonder (quite rightly) where forgiveness and justification fit into this. And so let me reassure you, Allen integrates it in his very next sentence, but he does so in a very helpful way: *"While justification is the ground of this participation in God, sanctifying fellowship is the goal of the gospel."*

We *are* justified by faith in Christ. It is a vital truth that we explored in issue 04. But God justified us for a purpose, namely to bring us back into "sanctifying fellowship." The ground of our relationship with God is our justification, and the goal of our salvation is our sanctification. Over the course of this issue of *Primer* I think we will see how true and helpful that is.

One of the great benefits will be to rehabilitate the idea of sanctification. Often it seems to Christians to be onerous – conjuring up ideas of joyless abstinence: the price we pay for being forgiven – and yet that is so far from the truth. As Allen says, sanctifying fellowship is the gracious gift of God. The Bible announces it to us as good news; the gospel of holiness.

To help us explore and proclaim that good news, we have a number of articles in this issue of *Primer*. To begin with, Dan Green lays out the terrain in a helpful interaction with several recent books on sanctification. Dan introduces a number of areas into which we then dig deeper.

The Old Testament is frequently overlooked when Christians write about sanctification, despite the fact that New Testament understandings of holiness owe so much to the Old. For that reason we asked Eric Ortlund to write up his thoughts on the way holiness is defined and expressed in the life of Israel and what that means for believers today.

For our historical text we have chosen an excerpt from Henry Scougal's *The Life of God in the Soul of Man*. It is a remarkable devotional text that helps us learn how to contemplate God's character and love, and how to be transformed by that contemplation. Tim Chester is our guide to that text, introducing and annotating it for us.

Next, I've written a piece on the significance of union with Christ for our holiness. That provides us with a chance to think about the nature of sanctification and the extent to which we are able to live holy lives in this present life.

As ever, our last two articles turn more to the practical application of our theme to ministry. In an evangelical culture that often speaks about the sanctifying power of private Bible study and prayer, and amidst growing enthusiasm for the transformative power of liturgy, we turn our attention to a couple of less well-travelled paths. First, Matthew Roberts makes a compelling argument for the importance of the gathered church to our growth in holiness, making great use of the Reformers and in critical dialogue with James K. A. Smith and his work on liturgical formation. Second, Julian Hardyman offers a wonderfully insightful and honest reflection on the sanctifying potential of suffering in ministry in the interview that closes this issue of *Primer*. He explores the close scriptural connection between suffering and sanctification, and helps us think how to minister out of our own suffering and how to help others to navigate theirs.

One last note: if you saw the advert for this issue in the last *Primer*, you will have seen Marcus Honeysett advertised as a contributor. We will not disappoint you! When we recently asked for feedback on *Primer*, one common suggestion was that we provide a more accessible article on the same topic as each issue of *Primer* that could serve church members well. Marcus has written that piece for us, and you can find it on **PrimerHQ.com**. So please feel free to circulate that widely, and keep the ideas coming for how we can serve you and your churches better (***info@primerhq.com***).

DAVID SHAW is the Editor of *Primer*. He is part-time Theological Adviser for FIEC and part-time lecturer in New Testament and Greek at Oak Hill Theological College, London. He's married to Jo and they have four children.

🐦 *@_david_shaw*

KEY

QUESTIONS

IN THE

CURRENT

DEBATES

Holiness matters.

>> It is what we have been saved for: *Christians have been chosen by God in Christ before the foundation of the world to be holy and blameless in his sight (Eph 1:4).*

>> It is what we are called to be: *God's people are commanded to be holy as he is holy (Lev 11:45, 19:2, 1 Pet 1:16).*

>> And it is vital that we are: *Without holiness we will not see the Lord (Heb 12:14).*

DAN GREEN is the pastor of Banstead Community Church, Surrey, and has been in this role for the last eight and a half years. He is married to Kate and they have three children.

🐦 *@blogofdan*

But what is holiness? And how does it relate to the language of sanctification?

To sanctify means 'to make holy' and Scripture teaches that this is something God has done, is doing, and will do. There is a past, present, and future tense to sanctification. Believers are sanctified; already holy. This is sometimes referred to as positional or definitive sanctification (Acts 20:32). We are also being sanctified progressively as we strive to live holy lives (2 Cor 3:18), and this continues throughout our lives until the moment our sanctification is perfected when we see Jesus face to face (1 Jn 3:2).

David Peterson captures both the definitive and progressive aspects to sanctification when he writes, *"Believers are definitively consecrated to God in order to live dedicated and holy lives, to his glory."*

David Peterson, *Possessed by God: A New Testament Theology of Sanctification and Holiness* (Leicester: Apollos, 1995), 27.

HOLINESS DEBATES

In recent years a whole host of concerns have been raised that we have neglected or misunderstood the doctrine of sanctification; in Kevin DeYoung's phrase, there is a *"hole in our holiness."* So where has this claim that holiness is not being taken seriously enough come from?

From the title of his book, *The Hole in our Holiness: Filling the Gap between Gospel Passion and the Pursuit of Holiness* (Wheaton Ill.: Crossway, 2012).

Within Calvinistic and Reformed circles, questions have been raised because of the influence of the 'New Calvinist' or 'Young, Restless, and Reformed' movement.

For more information on the New Calvinist Movement see Colin Hansen's *Young, Restless, Reformed* (Wheaton Ill.: Crossway, 2008), and assessments of it in Jeremy Walker, *The New Calvinism Considered* (London: Evangelical Press, 2013), and Josh Buice (ed.), *The New Calvinism: New Reformation or Theological Fad?* (Ross-shire: Christian Focus, 2017).

That is,
thinking that
our salvation
ultimately rests
on our obedience.

Some pastors and church leaders associated with this grouping have pushed back the boundaries of what was previously considered acceptable behaviour in the church, in the name of contextualisation, especially in areas such as entertainment, alcohol, fashion, and language used from the pulpit. Others have questioned the usefulness of the Ten Commandments, or the place of commands more generally, for fear of slipping into **legalism**.

These developments alone would be reason enough for revisiting the doctrine of sanctification, but alongside them there has also been much discussion around *how* we are made holy.

Steven J. Lawson,
"Holiness is
Relevant," in *The
New Calvinism:
New Reformation
of Theological
Fad?*, 83.

One view put forward most prominently by Tullian Tchividjian, Billy Graham's grandson and a former Presbyterian pastor, is that all you need to do to be made holy is *"look back and believe your justification"* as reflected in the following quotations:

Tullian Tchividjian, *Jesus + Nothing =
Everything* (Wheaton Ill.: Crossway, 2011),
now out of print, Kindle Edition, 95.

> *Sanctification is the daily hard work of going back to the reality of our justification. It's going back to the certainty of our objectively secured pardon in Christ and hitting the refresh button a thousand times a day.*

ibid. 78.

> *Growth in the Christian life is the process of receiving Christ's "It is finished" into new and deeper parts of our being every day, and it happens as the Holy Spirit daily carries God's good word of justification into our regions of unbelief – what one writer calls our "unevangelized territories."*

ibid. 175.

> *So, by all means work! But the hard work is not what you think it is – your personal improvement and moral progress. The hard work is washing your hands of you and resting in Christ's finished work for you, which will inevitably produce personal improvement and moral progress.*

Yet this goes against traditional understanding that sanctification happens when, by God's enabling grace, we are able *"more and more to die unto sin, and live unto righteousness"* as the Westminster Shorter Catechism puts it.

So how do we rightly balance the gift of grace and call to holiness? In the rest of this article I want to explore that question under two headings and with the help of five recent books.

The headings are *What is holiness?* and *How does holiness work?*

As for the five books, let me introduce them briefly:

Kevin DeYoung's *The Hole in our Holiness* and, more recently, *How Does Sanctification Work?* by David Powlison deal with the subject at a popular level. DeYoung is especially helpful in unpacking the place of effort in the Christian life, while avoiding the error of legalism, and Powlison in showing how sanctification actually takes place in real life situations.

Kevin DeYoung, *The Hole in our Holiness: Filling the Gap between Gospel Passion and the Pursuit of Holiness* (Wheaton Ill.: Crossway, 2012).

David Powlison, *How Does Sanctification Work?* (Wheaton Ill.: Crossway, 2017),

Devoted to God, ix.

Sinclair Ferguson's book *Devoted to God* aims, in his own words, *"to provide a manual of biblical teaching on holiness developed on the basis of extended expositions of foundation passages in the New Testament."* Ferguson's many years as a pastor shine through as he explains and applies the different passages, all the time showing how the gospel leads to a life of holiness by providing the strength and stimulus we need to obey what God commands.

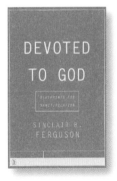

Sinclair Ferguson, *Devoted to God: Blueprints for Sanctification* (Edinburgh: Banner of Truth, 2016), ix.

Sanctification by Michael Allen is a volume in the *New Studies in Dogmatics* series and is more scholarly in type and broader in scope. He looks at how sanctification relates to other key doctrines (God, creation, covenant, and so on), along the way conversing with some of the church's most trusted theologians.

Michael Allen, *Sanctification* (New Studies in Dogmatics. Grand Rapids: Zondervan, 2017).

Finally, there is a helpful series of essays edited by Kelly M. Kapic in a book that also bears the title *Sanctification*. This volume wrestles with some of the more complex features of the doctrine, which is not surprising given that it is an edited collection of papers presented at an academic conference. There is a more uneven feel to it, with some of the essays more accessible than others.

Kelly M. Kapic ed., *Sanctification: Explorations in Theology and Practice*, (Downer's Grove Ill.: IVP, 2016).

1. WHAT IS HOLINESS?

There is a danger that in trying to describe what holiness is, we simply rehearse the implicit or explicit moral code of whatever generation or class we belong to. As Allen notes, *"much that has gone under the name of holiness has, in fact, been mere cultural preference."* We therefore first need to take a step back and understand what Scripture says about holiness and holy living before we can then apply principles to our specific context.

DeYoung is helpful here. See *The Hole in our Holiness*, 17, 34-35.

Allen, *Sanctification*, 21.

All the books mentioned above are broadly in agreement: in Scripture, holiness involves *separateness*. In describing God's separateness, Allen speaks of it in both a *metaphysical* (or *majestic*) sense and a *moral* sense: God is holy as One who is exalted above all his creation and is distinct from all he has made. God is also holy in that he is morally perfect and separate from sin, loving righteousness and hating all that is evil.

Whilst not denying these definitions of holiness, Ferguson argues that it is important to press beyond the language of separateness. He writes, *"For anything to be true of God as he is in himself, it must also be quite true apart from his work of creation."*

Ferguson, *Devoted to God*, 1-2.

From this viewpoint, God's holiness cannot be fully understood as separateness, since the Father, Son, and Holy Spirit were not separated from each other. He concludes that by holiness, *"We mean the perfectly pure devotion of each of these three persons to the other two."*

ibid. 2.

Devotion will obviously mean being separate from sin, but how does this square with God's holiness described as separateness in a metaphysical sense? Ferguson deals with this, by explaining that the eternal devotedness of the persons of the Trinity to each other is of such an intensity that creatures cannot bear it. The point is not that holiness does not involve separation but that this separation flows out of devotion to God. In the truest sense then, to be holy is to be as devoted to God as God is.

As in Isaiah 6.

And how can we know what that looks like? Well God has shown us. After all, the incarnate Son's earthly life exemplified the same devotion to his Father he has shown for all eternity. His food, he said, was to do the will of his Father.

To follow in Jesus' footsteps, then, is to be restored to true humanity, made in the image of God. But it is also to enter into the divine life of God as sons and daughters in the Son.

Derek Tidball's essay in *Sanctification* (Kapic) is a sermon about holiness as the restoring of God's image.

So that's what a holy life looks like. That's what holiness is. But how does it come about in a person's life? How does sanctification work?

For more on what holiness looks like in the Old Testament, see Eric Ortlund's article, starting on page 16.

2. HOW DOES HOLINESS WORK?

As we mentioned in the introduction, there is a definitive, once-for-all sense in which we have been sanctified. God has made his people holy. In the gospel, he shares his holiness with them in Christ. In this respect, sanctification is a gift. Making someone holy is a work that God has done. But it is also a work which he continues to do. God is *making* us holy.

As highlighted already, in discussions around the doctrine of sanctification some take the view that, for God to make us holy, all that needs to happen is for us to look to Christ and believe in our justification. Both Powlison and DeYoung challenge this 'silver bullet' approach.

Whilst agreeing that we are sanctified by remembering our justification, Powlison questions whether it is *"always the crucial ingredient in how we are progressively changed and sanctified."* He goes on to comment that

Powlison, *How Does Sanctification Work?*, 27.

ibid., 30. *"A vast Bible, centuries of pastoral experience, and innumerable testimonies bear joint witness that there is a lot more to it."* Then, by using case studies of how people have actually been changed more into Christ's image, he proposes that it occurs through the interplay of five factors: the direct intervention of God; the words of Scripture; the wisdom of other people; the circumstances of life; and the active personal participation in the change.

DeYoung's approach is slightly different. He describes Jesus as the Great Physician who prescribes a remedy consisting of different motivations and means that God uses to make his people holy. Particular truths from God's word will have a sanctifying effect on individuals according to their differing circumstances.

Thus there is good reason to think that there is no singular sanctifying silver bullet. The Bible's teaching is broader and more complex than that. In fact, it requires an understanding of how sanctification relates to several other areas.

We are going to briefly consider five of them:

2.1 SANCTIFICATION'S RELATIONSHIP TO JUSTIFICATION

It is important to recognise the difference between justification and sanctification. Justification is an objective declaration of our righteousness in God's sight, whereas sanctification is both an objective declaration that we have been made holy, but **also a subjective**
See Kapic, *Sanctification*, 13. **process of growing in holiness.**

Yet justification and sanctification are inexplicably linked. Justification is the grounds for our sanctification and sanctification inevitably follows. As Ferguson says,
Devoted to God, 9. *"It is not possible to be justified without being sanctified and then growing in holiness."*

However, we must not make the mistake of thinking that our sanctification, our becoming holy, contributes to our justification. Progress in Christlikeness is not meritorious in that way. This should be a great relief to us, and should actually encourage us to pursue godliness, knowing that our status of belonging to God is secure. Allen writes, *"Far from undercutting the call*
Sanctification, 188. *to holiness, the free gift of righteousness in Christ alone actually frees one for selfless, sacrificial service to others by orienting the Christian to find their hope and their life in Christ alone and outside of their own doing, working, achieving, or being."*

2.2 SANCTIFICATION'S RELATIONSHIP TO OUR UNION WITH CHRIST

The basis for our sanctification is our justification, and, like our justification, our sanctification is dependent upon our union with Christ, which we are brought into by faith. *"As the Holy Spirit unites us to Christ by faith, we receive both the free forgiveness of sins through the imputation of Christ's righteousness and new life to walk faithfully by God's sustaining grace in that freedom Christ has won for us."*

Brannon Ellis, 'Covenantal Union and Communion,' in Kapic ed., *Sanctification*, 84. For more on the significance of union with Christ, see David Shaw's article, starting on page 38.

In Christ, we have died to our old life in Adam where sin reigned, and have been raised to newness of life in him. Now, set free from slavery to sin, we are to live out our new identities by offering ourselves to God and our bodies to him as instruments of righteousness. It is a call to be who we now are in him, and this requires activity on our part, which is the next factor to consider.

2.3 SANCTIFICATION'S RELATIONSHIP TO HUMAN ACTIVITY

God makes his people holy. It is the Holy Spirit who conforms the believer to the image of Christ. But it is not the case that we are completely passive in that process. There is real activity on our part and we are not to make the mistake of thinking that all we have to do is *"let go and let God"* in order to be sanctified.

This was the teaching of the old Keswick Theology. For more on this see Andrew Naselli, *No Quick Fix: Where Higher Life Theology Came From, What It Is, and Why It's Harmful* (Bellingham, WA: Lexham, 2017).

Paul is clear that divine grace and human effort are involved in Phil 2:12-13, exhorting the church to *"work out your salvation with fear and trembling, for it is God who works in you to will and to act according to his good purpose."*

We work and he works. It is he who calls us to be holy before any desire is awakened to respond to what he has done. Not only that, but he has given us his Spirit to energise and work in us that which pleases him, ensuring that we will be holy and giving us the confidence, *"that he who began a good work in you will carry it on to completion until the day of Christ Jesus"* (Phil 1:6). **Thus there is divine grace before, and in, human activity.**

See chapter 9, 'Grace and Responsibility,' in Allen, *Sanctification*, 227-256.

'Sanctification by Faith?' in Kapic ed., *Sanctification*, 65.

So we can agree with Henri Blocher, when he writes, *"Our response counts for God – even though it comes from him and operates under his rule!"*

Sanctification involves looking to the Lord in faith and actively striving to be holy.

2.4 SANCTIFICATION'S RELATIONSHIP TO THE LAW

I take the view that the moral aspects of the Mosaic law are binding on believers. Even if someone disagrees with that, the New Testament commands of Jesus will function in a similar way to what I describe here.

A rejection of laws and commands, living anti-*nomos*, anti-law.

Richard Lints, 'Living by Faith – Alone? Reformed Responses to Antinomianism' in Kapic ed., *Sanctification*, 48-49. Those thoughts reflect the great announcements of Gal 3:13 and Rom 8:1 – we have been redeemed from the curse of law; there is now no condemnation for those who are in Christ Jesus.

In any discussion of sanctification, it is important that we are clear about what role the law plays, otherwise there is a real risk of falling into both the trappings of legalism and antinomianism.

We need to recognise, first of all, that the law *"no longer exercises its judicial function over the believer. It no longer accuses or rewards"* because *"justification has removed the weight of the law on believers"* so that now the *"consequences of disobeying or obeying is not punishment or reward, but rather dissatisfaction or satisfaction."*

Calvin speaks of three uses of the law: i) To convict us of sin, ii) to restrain evil, and iii) to show God's redeemed people how to live.

"The third use (being also the principal use, and more closely connected with its proper end) has respect to believers in whose hearts the Spirit of God already flourishes and reigns… It admonishes believers and urges them on in well-doing" (Institutes, 2.7.12-13).

Instead, its function, often termed as 'the third use of the law', is that of instructions for living a godly life which pleases him. The law can therefore be seen as a wonderful gift from a gracious God who doesn't leave his people scratching their heads, wondering how they show that they love him.

Allen further adds, that *"We need the Decalogue not only to apprise us of our lawful obligations, but we also need it to discern how far the Holy Spirit has advanced us in his work of sanctification and by how much we still fall short of that goal, lest we become secure and imagine that we have now done all that is required."*

Allen, *Sanctification*, 276. (*Decalogue*, i.e. the Ten Commandments)

Understood in this way, the law should be viewed as a blessing for our good, rather than a burden that weighs us down.

2.5 SANCTIFICATION'S RELATIONSHIP TO THE LOCAL CHURCH

Ligon Duncan, *twitter.com/LigonDuncan*, 17 Dec 2017, accessed 12 Jan 2018.

Finally, one other factor to consider is the role the local church plays in the sanctification of a Christian. Ligon Duncan tweeted that, *"Most of what the New Testament encourages us to do by way of sanctification can't be done apart from a local congregation.”* Ferguson agrees with Duncan's comment, when he writes, *“Sanctification was never intended to be an individualistic project.”*

Devoted to God, 109.

What role, then, should other believers play in our individual sanctification?

First, as Derek Tidball points out, *“holiness is relational, and no one can claim to be holy if they are isolated or insulated from others who name Christ as Lord.”* Being like Christ will mean relating *“to one another as he related to others.”*

Derek Tidball, 'Holiness: Restoring God's Image: A Homily on Colossians 3:5-17' in Kapic ed., *Sanctification*, 31.

So at the simplest level, relationships give us the opportunity to be holy. But they also give us support, encouraging us and spurring us on. This is especially needed when we are struggling to keep going in the faith. Then there are the times after we have failed our Lord, when we need them to reassure us by reminding us of forgiveness and a fresh start guaranteed when we confess our sins. **We also need them to point out to us, courageously and kindly, those areas where it is clear to everyone apart from ourselves that growth is required.**

For more on the ways in which the ministry of the church promotes sanctification, see Matthew Roberts' article on page 54.

Now, if we are to take seriously what holiness is and how holiness works, how should we respond as pastors and church leaders?

3. IMPLICATIONS

Let's reflect on four areas where our understanding of the doctrine of sanctification intersects with our ministry within the local church. These four areas are our own individual progress in holiness, our preaching, what we pray for, and our pastoral oversight of those under our care.

3.1 OUR PROGRESS

Our lives as church leaders, like those of all Christians, should be marked by growth in holiness.

However, we also have the added responsibilities, as those who are **called to set an example to the flock**, to be seen by them to be making progress ourselves and also to be modelling how they should be growing.

1 Tim 4:2, 1 Pet 5:3, Heb 13:7.

Recognising that other people will be observing us and will be affected by our lives, should cause us to give careful attention to the way we live and to the kind of example we are setting.

3.2 OUR PREACHING

The Hole in Our Holiness, 19.

Kevin DeYoung writes that, *"Pastors don't know how to preach the good news in their sermons and still strongly exhort churchgoers to cleanse themselves from every defilement of body and spirit."*

In our sermons, we will want to tell those listening to God's word, how they are to live in a way that pleases their Lord (after all, the Bible is full of commands) and also how it is possible to live in this way.

To do this well we need to have a clear grasp of what holiness is, otherwise the way we describe the Christian life will cover all the 'safe' applications but fail to deal with 'respectable' sins and the broader scope of obedience required. The latter includes those areas that generally don't get much airtime in our preaching such as greed, laziness, not caring for widows, or complaining and grumbling.

We also need to have an appreciation of the dynamics of sanctification so that we don't limit our explanation of how a person grows in Christlikeness to one single factor.

3.3 OUR PRAYING

See especially Phil 1:9-11, Col 1:9-15, 2 Thess 1:11-12.

When you read through the prayers of the apostle Paul recorded in the New Testament, one of the prominent themes is his concern for the sanctification of the believers in the local churches to which he is writing. Paul **frequently prays** that these Christians will live godly lives and that God will give to them everything that they need in order for this to happen.

This presents us with a challenge regarding both our private and public prayers.

Are we praying individually for those in the congregation that they may *"live a life worthy of the Lord and may please him in every way"* (Col 1:10) or that God would make their *"love increase and overflow for each other and for everyone else"* (1 Thess 3:12) or that they *"will not do anything wrong"* (2 Cor 13:7)?

Are we leading the church when she gathers for corporate prayer to pray *"for [our] love to abound more and more in knowledge and depth of insight so that [we] may be able to discern what is best and may be pure and blameless until the day of Christ, filled with the fruit of righteousness that comes through Jesus Christ – to the glory and praise of God."* (Phil 1:9-11).

3.4 OUR PASTORAL CARE

One final area that our beliefs regarding sanctification will affect is that of pastoral care.

In exercising pastoral oversight of those under our care we need to treat attitudes and actions which are sinful seriously; rebuking, correcting and following a biblical process of church discipline when there is no repentance. A good understanding of true holiness will be vital in enabling us to differentiate between what is impure in God's sight and what is not, even if this runs counter to current cultural norms.

It will also give us a right expectation about how holy people will actually become in this life. Whilst we should expect them to show progressive change, this will often be slow and rather than getting frustrated, we must be patient and encourage them to go on striving for holiness.

Questions for further thought and discussion

1. What questions do you think people in your church have about sanctification? Reflect on the ways holiness or sanctification are spoken about, illustrated and encouraged. What is communicated implicitly by the culture of the church and the lifestyle of its members?

2. *"Sanctification is the daily hard work of going back to the reality of our justification. It's going back to the certainty of our objectively secured pardon in Christ and hitting the refresh button a thousand times a day."* Why do you think that approach is persuasive to many people? What does it helpfully guard against, and what are its limitations?

3. Apart from Phil 2:12-13, how would you start to prove to someone that our sanctification is God's work and also requires our effort? How could we tell if we have got the relationship between God's work and ours wrong?

4. How would you express the role of the Old Testament law in promoting our holiness? How would you defend that view?

5. In which of the areas that Dan outlines at the end of the article do you most want to develop? What action could you take to make a start on that?

God's holiness amongst his people in the Old Testament

"AS I AM HOLY"

In a justly famous passage from 1 Peter, the apostle makes a moving appeal for Christians to lead holy lives:

ERIC ORTLUND is a tutor in Hebrew and Old Testament at Oak Hill College, London. He previously taught at Briercrest College and Seminary (Canada) and studied at the University of Edinburgh.

🐦 *@EricNelsOrtlund*

1 Pet 1:13-19

Therefore, with minds that are alert and fully sober, set your hope on the grace to be brought to you when Jesus Christ is revealed at his coming. As obedient children, do not conform to the evil desires you had when you lived in ignorance. But just as he who called you is holy, so be holy in all you do; for it is written: "Be holy, because I am holy."

Since you call on a Father who judges each person's work impartially, live out your time as foreigners here in reverent fear. For you know that it was not with perishable things such as silver or gold that you were redeemed from the empty way of life handed down to you from your ancestors, but with the precious blood of Christ, a lamb without blemish or defect.

It is a passage that drips with Old Testament language: redemption, a spotless lamb, living as foreigners in exile. And at the heart of the passage Peter quotes from Leviticus, forcing our attention back to the Old Testament language of holiness.

One doesn't have to read long in the OT before seeing how frequently that language is found: the Hebrew root *qadash*, "to be holy," and its derivatives, are found almost 250 times in the Pentateuch alone, and recur through historical and prophetic literature. Surveying this theme as it clusters in the Bible's first five books will show some striking emphases and associations which Christians seeking to obey 1 Peter 1 might not be aware of. Although the way in which holiness is expressed and guarded in the old covenant is significantly different from how new covenant believers are sanctified, attention to the sometimes-strange use of holiness in the OT will greatly help Christians trying to conduct themselves well in the time of their exile, mindful of at what great cost their redemption was won.

THE HOLY GOD AND HIS WONDERS: HOLINESS AND THE EXODUS FROM EGYPT

The first reference to holiness in the OT is found in Gen 2:3, when God sanctifies the seventh day, because on it he rested. One of the many striking aspects about this first act of sanctification is that it is not revealed until the Mosaic covenant – although God himself keeps Sabbath at the beginning of creation, there is no indication that any of the Patriarchs kept Sabbath or even knew of it until God commanded it through Moses (Exod 20:8-11, Deut 5:12-15). Adding to the interest of this passage is the fact that God keeps the Sabbath commandment before commanding anyone else to – a point to which we'll return below.

Aside from the significant sanctification of the seventh day, the "holiness" word-group does not recur in any significant way in the book of Genesis. Although Abraham builds an altar in the land not his own (Gen 12:7), and Jacob is appropriately shaken when he realises he has been sleeping at the gate of heaven (Gen 28:16-17), neither Abraham's altar nor the site where Jacob sleeps is described as holy. The holiness of God does not come into play at this early stage of redemptive history.

This changes with the book of Exodus, which is saturated with the language of holiness, especially in the instructions for building the tabernacle (chs. 25-31) and the tabernacle's construction (chs. 35-40). The first mention of holiness occurs in a significant way in an earlier chapter, however. It's a normal day at work for Moses (3:1) when he notices a bush on fire, but the leaves are still green and the bark uncharred (v. 2). As Moses gets close, however, God tells him not to draw near without taking off his sandals, because the ground is holy (v. 5). We learn that God's presence "contaminates" physical space when he appears visibly on earth and makes it holy like God himself. (The command to take off his sandals is probably to prevent the mixing of normal soil with holy – a more tactile and concrete reason than many Christians realise – such mixture being a persistent problem throughout Leviticus and Numbers.)

This first encounter between Moses and the ancestral Israelite God on holy ground is also significant because we see in it the entire trajectory of Exodus and Leviticus in miniature. Looking further ahead in Exodus, God frees his people from slavery (Exod 14-15) and seals them in a covenant relationship with himself (24:1-11). A home is then built for the new husband and wife to live in. Exodus 25-40 shows the preparation of the tabernacle as a fit place for God's name to indwell; the book of Leviticus shows how the other partner in the covenant can come into God's presence. And Leviticus will continually use the verb "draw near," as in Exod 3:5, to speak of Israelites offering sacrifice in the tabernacle (some 126 times, and eight times in chapter 1 alone). This prompts us to read God's warning *not* to "draw near" to the holy ground of the burning bush in a slightly different way – although Moses cannot draw near unprepared, God's intention in the next two books for Moses and all Israel is just exactly for them to draw near to his presence. God's holiness cannot be taken lightly; but the restrictions about who can draw near and when, as laid out in Leviticus, all stand in the service of God's intention that his people not just look on his holiness from afar (which in itself would be more than they could ask for) but come within the sphere of God's holiness and participate in it: *"I am the Lord who sanctifies you"* (Lev 20:8). This is part of the "good news" of Exodus, and God's larger intention in the Pentateuch is already present in the burning bush encounter.

At this point, we are far enough along in the biblical story that we should pause and reflect on what holiness actually means. The word is never explicitly defined, but the way in which the theme is handled shows that holiness in the Pentateuch implies separateness and also moral purity: persons, times, or objects are holy in that they are set apart for special use in God's service and not common use, and must remain clean and/or morally pure in that use. It is easy to see the reflection of God's character here. God exists not as part of the world, but is transcendently "set apart," entirely in his own category; and he does so as a radiantly pure being, in absolute contrast to creation after the fall. From this perspective, to say, "God is holy" is tantamount to saying "God is God." Holiness is God's inner nature which he possesses as the only God.

A third aspect of holiness, in addition to "separateness" and "purity," is wholeness or beauty (in fact, the English word "holiness" is related to the word "wholeness"). This is seen in small ways, such as the requirement that animals to be sacrificed must be whole of body (Lev 1:3) and that priests who serve must be the same (Lev 21:16-23). It is also seen in the command to *"worship the Lord in the beauty of holiness"* (Ps 29:2, 96:9). This is important because it shows that holiness is no abstraction. There is something radiant, glorious, and beautiful about God's holiness; but because it is divine holiness, it is also terrifying. This explains Israel's paradoxical attraction and fear at Mt. Sinai: on the one hand, barriers must be set up lest the people get too close (19:21; in v. 23, these barriers sanctify/set apart the mountain); on the other hand, they find God's voice and presence unbearable and feel they will die (20:19). God's holiness is completely overwhelming to human beings and profoundly attractive at the same time.

Even in modern translation, the language surrounding holiness in the Pentateuch can sound archaic and even barbaric. But I believe Yahweh's gracious revelation of his holiness and guidance of Israel to participate in it touches on desires deep inside every human heart. That longing after a beauty which exists outside the world but can perhaps break in on it; for a purity untouched by the natural pattern of decay and death; for a wholeness transcending the inner divisions of the human psyche or society – one doesn't have to read fiction or watch films for very long before these kinds of yearnings surface. Romantic relationships are depicted in a way which grace their participants with a kind of transcendent purity, or the hero wins a victory which restores wholeness to a community and unifies them. When the Lord says to Israel, *"I am the Lord who sanctifies you,"* he is fulfilling a cluster of desires which lie very deep within us. As C. S. Lewis said, *"We do not want merely to see beauty, though, God knows, even that is bounty enough. We want something else which can hardly be put into words – to be united with the beauty we see, to pass into it, to receive it into ourselves, to bath in it, to become part of it."*

"The Weight of Glory," in *C. S. Lewis Essay Collection: Faith, Christianity and the Church* (London: Harper Collins, 2000), 104.

The example of a hero acting on behalf of a community in the above paragraph may seem a strange one to raise in a discussion of holiness. But we learn from Exod 15:11, as Moses and the nation praise God for the exodus, that holiness is not static: *"Who is like you, Lord, among the gods? Who is like you, majestic in holiness, fearsome in praises, working miracles?"* The transcendent uniqueness of God – that he exists entirely in his own category – is clearly present in this verse, together with his majesty, glory, and divine beauty. Significantly, however, divine holiness is now joined to his saving action on his people's behalf. The last word of the verse is often (not wrongly) translated "wonders," but I believe the stronger word "miracles" better captures how God steps in to rescue helpless people from disaster. The reference to God's "holy abode" two verses later in v. 13 deepens the reader's grasp of God's holiness by showing that the exodus is not an occasional act which leaves God's people vulnerable to further exploitation: since this "abode" is the sanctuary (see v. 17), vv. 13-18 show God completing the victory of the exodus by leading the people he has redeemed and "planting" them there. The holy ground Moses stumbled upon, Israel is now established upon, never to leave.

SANCTIFIED PLACE, SANCTIFIED MINISTERS: THE TABERNACLE

At this point in the book of Exodus, "holiness" has not recurred in the text with great frequency, even though its few uses are highly significant. Once Israel reaches Sinai and is sealed in their covenant relationship with the Lord in chs. 19-24, however, this changes. As the various dimensions and articles of the tabernacle are commanded (chs. 25-31) and then constructed (chs. 35-40), everything in the tabernacle is described as holy in one way or another. This is most clearly seen at the end of ch. 31, as it is specified that everything in the tabernacle, from the outer courtyard and the altar of burnt offering, to the holy place with its furniture (the table with the bread of the presence, the Menorah, and the incense altar), and even the most holy place with the ark of the covenant, must be anointed with oil mixed with the finest of spices (Exod 30:22-28) so that it might become most holy (v. 29). This command is carried in 40:9-11, after which the divine glory fills the tabernacle so intensely that not even Moses can enter (v. 35). That the text specifies that it is the glory of the Lord which fills the newly-complete tabernacle and not his holiness should not surprise, because the Old Testament shows God's glory as simply the manifestation or outward expression of his holiness. (As Isaiah 6:3 says, *"Holy, holy, holy is the Lord of hosts; the whole earth is full of his glory"*). Glory is holiness revealed. Significantly, the instructions for the consecration of the altar of burnt offering in the courtyard specify that it is sanctified for God's glory (Exod 29:43).

As with the place, so with the people ministering there: Aaron and his sons are to be consecrated for service in the tabernacle (Exod 29:44, 30:30), as well as the clothes they wear (Exod 28:3-4, 41; 29:1, 27; 40:13). Even the plate on Aaron's turban has "holy to the Lord" written on it as he bears any guilt from the worshippers (Exod 28:36, 38). The ordination of Aaron and his sons in Leviticus 8 involves applying the blood of a sacrificial ram to the lobe of their right ear, their right thumb, and the big toe of their right foot (Lev 8:23), three extremities which symbolise the totality of the priest's body and person set apart for service in God's tabernacle. Elsewhere, Leviticus says that, because the priests bring offerings near, they are to be most holy to the Lord (Lev 21:6), made holy by God for their service (Lev 21:15, 23; 22:9, 16, 23). In fact, Lev 21:8 ties the sanctification of the priest, who brings offerings near, to God's sanctification of the entire people; the holy God binds a holy people to himself through holy priests. Holiness pervades not just the priests' work at the altar, but their teaching as well, as they help Israelites

"Altars," *Dictionary of the Old Testament: Pentateuch* (Nottingham, IVP: 2003), 35.

distinguish between holy and common, clean and unclean (that is, pure and mixed; Lev 10:10-11). Even the animals the priests sacrifice are called holy (Exod 29:27, 33, 36, 37; Lev 2:2, 10).

Sacred time is another important dimension of how the holiness of God's presence among his people is expressed. This is most obviously seen in the Sabbath, which Israel is to remember, in order to sanctify it (Exod 20:8-11, 31:13; Deut 5:12). The Sabbath is not just a day to relax; it is a different quality of time, when Israel participated in the victorious peace God first enjoyed before the fall, after creation was finished. Other sacred assemblies in Israel's liturgical year are consecrated, such as Passover (Exod 12:16, Lev 23:4) and Jubilee (Lev 25:10).

We should remember the full significance of holiness as we read of the sanctification of the whole of the tabernacle and the priests who work there. God's real presence is located in the most holy place, above the mercy seat, in between the cherubim. *"I will make my dwelling* [literally, my tabernacle] *among you, and my soul shall not abhor you. I will walk among you and will be your God, and you shall be my people"* (Lev 26:11-12). As a result, the sanctuary exists entirely set apart to God and his service; unlike the rest of creation, it is utterly pure and clean, subject to no pollution or corruption. It is also beautiful, *"the joy of the whole earth"* (Ps 48:2), *"the perfection of beauty"* (Ps 50:2). Little wonder David spoke so strongly about loving the temple, where God's glory dwells (Ps 26:8), or that pilgrims longed to reach their destination there (Ps 84:2). Those serving there truly are blessed (84:4). It is the one place psalmists want to be, because, as the place of God's presence, it is the one place of life, safety, and joy (see especially Ps 5:7, 20:2, 23:6, 36:8, 61:4, 63:2, 92:12-13). This perspective is complemented by the book of Leviticus, which draws a massive contrast between the outside world as the place of uncleanness, violence, and death, and the sanctuary as the one place of life and flourishing. Although speaking specifically of the altar of burnt offering, L. D. Hawk's comment could apply equally to the whole sanctuary: it *"marked the intersection of the mystical and the material, a site where transitions and transactions could take place between the ordinary world of human experience and the holy sphere that marked the divine world."*

THE DANGERS OF HOLINESS AND THE NEED TO PROTECT IT

The massive gift which the holy place represents is by now hopefully clear. One need not read far in Pentateuch literature, however, to realise that although God's holiness is unchanging, the holiness of the places and people he sanctifies is vulnerable and must be protected. This is seen most dramatically in the day of atonement in Leviticus 16, when the sanctuary is ritually cleansed from all the impurities which the year's worship had accidentally accumulated (vv. 16-17, 19). The day of atonement represents the high point of the year's atoning activities and the one day of the year when the high priest enters the most holy place to sprinkle blood – but not without incense, lest he die (v. 13).

The danger of death because of God's holy presence in the tabernacle is never absent from Exodus-Deuteronomy. This is most tragically evident in the initial consecration of Aaron and his sons to the priesthood and the dramatic acceptance of their offerings (Lev 9:22-24), which leads Nadab and Abihu to presumptuously draw near unprotected by the sacrifices God has commanded (10:1) – and the fire which previously devoured the sacrifices (9:24) devours them (10:2). God is determined to defend his holiness as he dwells with his people; when Israelites draw near without sacrifice, they become their own sacrifice to maintain God's holiness. The terrible responsibility of priests to guard the Lord's holiness is clear in **v. 3**: *"Among those who draw near me, I will be sanctified, and before the face of the people, I will be glorified"* (note again the connection between God's holiness and the outward display of this glory). "Those who draw near" are priests, who must minister in accordance with God's holiness, so that his glory is not diminished among the laity. The same issue surfaces when Moses is tragically excluded from the promised land in Num 20:2-13: although his deviation from the Lord's instructions seems small, it amounts to not trusting God in such a way that fails to uphold God's holiness in the sight of the people (v. 12). For this reason, Moses is excluded from the promised land. Tragically, God shows himself holy in the waters of Meribah (v. 13) – but not in such a way that Moses benefits from it. An obedient Israel will benefit from God's holy presence in profound ways, but disobedience in God's people means that God asserts his holiness at their expense. This is not cruel on God's part; since God's holiness is his God-ness, a failure on God's part to maintain or uphold his own holiness would amount to un-God-ing himself.

My translation.

Less dramatic examples of the danger of contact with holy things are scattered throughout the Pentateuch. Because anyone touching anything in the sanctuary becomes holy by contact (Exod 30:29), disposal of the remains of sacrifice become more complicated (in Lev 6:11, the priest must change clothes). Any priest touching any holy thing while in an unclean state loses his ministry (Lev 22: 3), and any priest or layperson who eats of the fellowship offering while ritually unclean is cut off (Lev 7:20, that is, exiled from the people [Lev 18:26-29]). God's holy presence in the midst of an unclean world complicates life in countless ways. Because God is physically present with his people under the terms of the old covenant, physical purity and spiritual purity overlap.

But not for the priests only – although Aaron and his sons are specially set apart, the entirety of the people are called a holy nation in Exod 19:6: In Exod 22:31, it is because all the people are holy that anything torn by wild beasts is not to be eaten (remember that since holiness is associated with wholeness, a torn body tarnishes the holiness of the eater). All of Israel are to consecrate themselves to the Lord (Lev 11:44). This command is repeated in Lev 20:7-8, a chapter intended to keep Israel separate from the surrounding nations by preventing them from imitating their practices and especially sexual sin (vv. 10-21). This is made explicit in v. 25: *"I am the Lord your God, who has separated you from the peoples."* All of the laws of Exodus-Deuteronomy are intended to keep Israel safe in the realm of the Lord's holiness and life. This helps to explain some of the laws which are strange to modern Christians. Bruce Waltke writes,

An Old Testament Theology (Grand Rapids: Zondervan, 2007), 468.

The Israelites were commanded not to mix seeds or crops and not to mix different types of cloth in sewing. Therefore, the theme of purity was worked into the everyday life of the Israelites and safeguarded them from mixing their human seed with pagans. These purity laws inculcated the notion of holiness so that Israel would learn that they were to be a pure people, set apart for God.

HOLINESS IN THE ESCHATOLOGICAL AGE

There is a great deal more that could be said about holiness in the Pentateuch, and indeed in the rest of the OT. But one expression of the theme of holiness in later parts of the OT which should not be omitted is the eschatological re-assertion of the Lord's holiness at the end of this age and the re-sanctification of creation. Ezekiel the priest (Ezek 1:3) expresses this hope repeatedly in his book. When God brings his people back from exile, cleanses them of their idolatry, and once again accepts their worship (Ezek 20:40-41), God will manifest his holiness before the sight of all the nations (v. 42; see also 36:23, 39:27). Part of Israel's renewed life in the promised land after the exile involves all the nations knowing that the Lord is the one sanctifying Israel as he makes his sanctuary in their midst (37:28). Hard on the heels of this comes the eschatological battle, which the Lord coordinates so that he might vindicate his holiness in his victory against Gog and Magog and the whole world might know him (38:16, 23). Ezekiel ends his text with a long description of the eschatological temple (chs. 40-48) in the city named *Yahweh shama*, "The Lord is There" (48:35). Zechariah expresses the same by prophesying that, one day, every pot not just inside the temple but in the city as a whole will have "Holy to the Lord" written on it (14:20-21), a way of communicating that the distinction between holy and common will be obliterated and everything will be holy. Isaiah adds his voice to this chorus by promising that "on that day," even a foreigner and eunuch will be accepted in God's service in the temple (Isa 56.3-8) – those formerly excluded (Lev 21.17-21) are now included.

This prophetic hope finds wonderful fulfilment in the New Testament not just in the new creation, where nothing unclean can enter the holy city (Rev. 21.27), but also in Jesus' earthly ministry, as those who would have been ritually unclean are now healed. The defensive and protective measures of the Mosaic code fall away in Jesus' ministry. N.T. Wright puts it this way:

N.T. Wright, "Jesus, Israel, and the Cross," *SBL Seminar Papers* 1985, 83.

Jesus' entire public ministry is actually a fulfilment of what the temple symbolised. He forgives sins directly, apart from sin offerings, guilt offerings, and the ritual of the Day of Atonement. He touches the unclean, lepers, and corpses, and is touched by the unclean, the woman with the haemorrhage, and remarkably uncleanness does not win by contaminating Jesus, but instead the unclean becomes clean. Jesus... enters the house of Zacchaeus and according to Jewish law thus contracts uncleanness, but when he emerges from Zacchaeus' house to face the accusing crowd, it is not he who is unclean but Zaccheaus who is a "son of Abraham."

It has been pointed out that, in Genesis 1, God describes everything as very good (1:31), but the only thing described as holy is the Sabbath – which no human yet knows about or keeps. Although creation is flawless and exactly according to God's specifications, it is not yet holy. But just as God himself is the first person to keep his own rules about holiness before commanding humans to participate, so God himself takes the vulnerable holiness of one part of creation in the Pentateuch and expands it so that all creation is sanctified.

HOLINESS IN THE OLD TESTAMENT AND SANCTIFIED CHRISTIANS

Christians may read the numerous chapters of the Pentateuch devoted to protecting God's holiness and breathe a sigh of relief they were not born under the old covenant. The New Testament will sometimes echo a similar sentiment; Hebrews 12:18-24 contrasts the terrifying appearance of God on Mt. Sinai with the heavenly Zion to which new covenant believers can draw near. Additionally, the NT is clear that physical or ritual cleanness no longer has the importance it did under the old covenant; because, in the new covenant, God dwells with his people spiritually and not physically (that is, by the outpoured Holy Spirit), the manner in which God's people must remain holy changes (even if the command remains). But this in no way means studying Exodus-Deuteronomy is fruitless for Christians.

Jay Sklar, who teaches Old Testament at Covenant Seminary in America and is an expert on Leviticus, had a class in which he required students to keep every law from Leviticus they could for one week and record their experience. Although some complaints were registered, Sklar summaries the student journals in the following way:

Sklar's commentary on Leviticus is excellent: Jay Sklar, *Leviticus* (TOTC; Nottingham, IVP 2014).

"Four Things That Happen When You Study Leviticus More Than 10 Years," available at thegospelcoalition.org, last accessed on 27/1/18.

> *Every day, I found myself focused on thinking about ritual purity and impurity. Partway through the week, I realized that I was thinking about these things **all day long and in every aspect of my life**, and that's when it hit me: God cares a lot about our purity and holiness. Not just from a ritual perspective, but also from a moral perspective. **All day long and in every aspect of life**, the Lord wants me to pursue purity in my heart, in my life, in my actions. He wants me to reflect his holiness in all that I do. I have been treating holiness way too lightly! O Lord, help me to be holy!*

Sklar comments, *"That's the kind of prayer you begin to pray when you soak in Leviticus."*

Familiarity with Leviticus helps Christians in another way. When we keep in mind the immense labour which went into the tabernacle's construction, daily operation, and defence against impurity, as well as the immense significance of being able to draw near and worship and the danger of drawing near without proper sacrifice, then the glory of Jesus Christ, the lamb of God and our great high priest, becomes deeply meaningful. He is the mediator who is able *"to save to the uttermost those who draw near to God through him"* (Heb 7:25), our great high priest, who is *"holy, innocent, unstained, separated from sinners, and exalted above the heavens"* (v. 26). Christians can draw near with confidence in a way only the high priest could do once a year (Heb 10:19-22). Not only that, the commands of the NT for Christians to remain holy take on great traction when their OT background is kept in mind. If my body is a temple of the Holy Spirit (1 Cor 6:19) and meant for the Lord (v. 13), how could I let sin reign in my mortal body (Rom 6:12-13)? As a member of God's holy priesthood (1 Pet 2:9), how could I do anything else but abstain from those passions warring against my soul (v. 12), hating even the garment stained by flesh (Jude 23)?

Studying the laws – which are no longer binding on new covenant believers but still help us understand our relationship with the Lord who sanctifies us – will repay careful attention. But this commandment is not burdensome, because the one who will make all creation holy like the tabernacle (Rev 22:5) also sanctifies us (1 Cor 1:2). Just as nothing becomes holy without God's presence and work, so God ultimately works his holiness into us as we obey.

Questions for further thought and discussion

1. Towards the start of the article, Eric writes: *"Although the way in which holiness is expressed and guarded in the old covenant is significantly different from how new covenant believers are sanctified, attention to the sometimes-strange use of holiness in the OT will greatly help Christians trying to conduct themselves well."*

   How has the article helped you grasp the continuity and discontinuity between the old covenant and the new? How does holiness look and work differently now? How is it similar?

2. Is it enough to say that holiness means "separate"? How does Eric encourage us to start enriching our definition? What pastoral and apologetic benefits might that have?

3. When people try to ridicule the OT prohibitions about mixing crops or fabrics, how could we best respond using this article?

4. What might a sermon or Bible study series on holiness in the OT look like? In light of this article, what might be the fruit of that in the life of the church?

THE LIFE OF GOD IN THE SOUL OF MAN

An extract from Henry Scougal's work, with an introduction and annotations by Tim Chester

TIM CHESTER is a faculty member of Crosslands Training, the pastor of Grace Church, Boroughbridge, in North Yorkshire, and the author of a number of books.

🐦 *@timchestercouk*

From a 1769 sermon, quoted in Michael A. G. Haykin, editor, *The Revived Puritan: The Spirituality of George Whitefield* (Dundas, Ontario: Joshua Press, 2000), 25-26.

"

When I was sixteen years of age, I began to fast twice a week for thirty-six hours together, prayed many times a day, received the sacrament every Lord's day, fasting myself almost to death all the forty days of Lent, during which I made a point of duty never to go less than three times a day to public worship, besides seven times a day to my private prayers. Yet I knew no more that I was to be born again in God, born a new creature in Christ Jesus, than if I were never born again... I must bear testimony to my old friend Mr Charles Wesley; he put a book into my hands called **The Life of God in the Soul of Man***, whereby God showed me, that I must be born again, or be damned.*

So wrote George Whitefield. *The Life of God in the Soul of Man*, which had proved so formative for Whitefield, was written by Henry Scougal, originally in the form of correspondence. Scougal died of tuberculosis in 1678 – he was just 28 years old. Four years earlier, he had been appointed Professor of Divinity at Aberdeen University.

At a time of widespread nominal Christianity, *The Life of God in the Soul of Man* is at pains to distinguish between true and false religion. **As Jim Packer notes**, Scougal could have focused more on the objective nature of Christ's work. But Scougal could assume this. His concern was to expose mere formal assent and external performance by constantly emphasising the inward transformation that the Spirit brings in true believers. His emphasis on the affections remains an important antidote to mere intellectualism. But *The Life of God in the Soul of Man* is not simply an exposé of nominal Christianity. Scougal goes on to show how true religion is to be cultivated in those born again by the Spirit of God.

Jim Packer, 'Introduction,' *The Life of God in the Soul of Man* (Christian Focus, 1996), 12.

Wonderfully, he knows that his challenging portrayal of true Christianity can make believers anxious, and so Scougal comes in with encouragement and help:

The Works of the Rev. Henry Scougal, 41.

See Num 13:26-33

Desponding thoughts may arise in the minds of those persons who begin to conceive somewhat more of the nature and excellency of religion than before. They have spied the land, and seen that it is exceeding good, that it flows with milk and honey; but they find they have the children of Anak to grapple with, many powerful lusts and corruptions to overcome, and they fear they shall never prevail against them. But why should we give way to such discouraging suggestions? Why should we entertain such unreasonable fears, which damp our spirits and weaken our hands, and augment the difficulties of our way? Let us encourage ourselves, my dear friend, let us encourage ourselves with those mighty aids we are to expect in this spiritual warfare; for greater is he that is for us, than all that rise up against us.

The Works of the Rev. Henry Scougal, 62.

The excerpt we are about to read comes near the end of the work. In this section, Scougal is suggesting *"some particular subjects of meditation"* in order to foster *"that lively faith which is the foundation of religion, the spring and root of the divine life."*

EXCERPT FROM *THE LIFE OF GOD IN THE SOUL OF MAN*

The text is freely available online. Headings have been added and Scougal's language has been lightly modernised.

I shall mention but two other means for begetting that holy and divine temper of spirit which is the subject of the present discourse. And **the first is** a deep and serious consideration of the truths of our religion, both as to the certainty and importance of them. The assent which is ordinarily given to divine truth is very faint and languid, very weak and ineffectual, flowing only from a blind inclination to follow that religion which is in fashion, or a lazy indifference and unconcernedness whether things be so or not. Men are unwilling to quarrel with the religion of their country, and since all their neighbours are Christians, they are content to be so too: but they are seldom at the pains to consider the evidences of those truths, or to ponder the importance and tendency of them; and thence it is that they have so little influence on their affections and practice. Those "spiritless and paralytic thoughts," (as someone rightly terms them,) are not able to move the will, and direct the hand.

The second means, which Scougal discusses later in this work, is "fervent and hearty prayer", *The Works of the Rev. Henry Scougal*, 72.

Scougal has in mind the notional beliefs of nominal Christians. We see this alternative to true religion less and less in our secular culture. But the challenge to be people of conviction remains – especially in the face of intolerance. Sanctification takes place when the truths of the gospel move from our heads to our hearts so that they "ravish our affections," as Scougal will later say. That is achieved by "a deep and serious consideration of the truth of our religion."

FROM HEAD TO HEART

We must, therefore, endeavour to work up our minds to a serious belief and full persuasion of divine truths, to a sense and feeling of spiritual things: our thoughts must dwell upon them till we be both convinced of them, and deeply affected with them. Let us urge forward our spirits, and make them approach the visible world, and fix our minds upon immaterial things, till we clearly perceive that these are no dreams; nay, that all things are dreams and shadows beside them. When we look about us, and behold the beauty and magnificence of this godly frame, the order and harmony of the whole creation, let our thoughts from thence take their flight towards that omnipotent wisdom and goodness which did at first produce, and does still establish and uphold the same.

When we reflect upon ourselves, let us consider that we are not a mere piece of organised matter, a curious and well-contrived engine; that there is more in us than flesh, and blood, and bones, even a divine spark, capable to know, and love, and enjoy our Maker; and though it be now exceedingly clogged with its dull and lumpish companion, yet ere long it shall be delivered, and can subsist without the body, as well as that can do without the clothes which we throw off at our pleasure. Let us often withdraw our thoughts from this earth, this scene of misery, and folly, and sin, and raise them towards that more vast and glorious world, whose innocent and blessed inhabitants solace themselves eternally in the divine presence, and know no other passions, but an unmixed joy and an unbounded love. And then consider how the blessed Son of God came down to this lower world to live among us, and die for us, that he might bring us to a portion of the same felicity; and think how he has overcome the sharpness of death, and opened the kingdom of heaven to all believers, and is now set down on the right hand of the Majesty on high, and yet is not the less mindful of us, but receives our prayers, and presents them to his Father, and is daily visiting his church with the influences of his Spirit, as the sun reaches us with his beams.

We might wonder whether Scougal is too negative towards the body, "our lumpish companion." But then Scougal might wonder whether we are too focused on the things of the earth and have stopped setting our hearts on things above, where Christ is (Col 3:10).

The serious and frequent consideration of these, and such other divine truths, is the most proper method to beget that lively faith which is the foundation of religion, the spring and root of the divine life. Let me further suggest some particular subjects of meditation for producing the several branches of it.

CONTEMPLATE GOD'S GLORY

To inflame our souls with the love of God, **let us consider the excellency of his nature, and his love and kindness towards us**. It is little we know of the divine perfections; and yet that little may suffice to fill our souls with admiration and love, to ravish our affections, as well as to raise our wonder; for we are not merely creatures of sense, that we should be incapable of any other affection but that which enters by the eyes. The character of any excellent person whom we have never seen, will many times engage our hearts, and make us hugely concerned in all his interests.

And what is it, I pray you, that engages us so much to those with whom we converse? I cannot think that is merely the colour of their face, in their comely proportions, for then we should fall in love with statues, and pictures, and flowers. These outward accomplishments may a little delight the eye, but would never be able to prevail so much on the heart, if they did not represent some vital perfection. We either see or apprehend some greatness of mind, or vigour of spirit, or sweetness of disposition; some sprightliness, or wisdom, or goodness, which charm our spirit and command our love. Now these perfections are not obvious to the sight, the eyes can only discern the signs and effects of them; and if it be the understanding that directs our affection, and vital perfections prevail with it, certainly the excellencies of the divine nature (the traces whereof we cannot but discover in everything we behold) would not fail to engage our hearts, if we did seriously view and regard them.

Shall we not be infinitely more transported with that almighty wisdom and goodness which fills the universe, and displays itself in all the parts of the creation, which establishes the frame of nature, and turns the mighty wheels of Providence, and keeps the world from disorder and ruin, than with the faint rays of the very same perfections which we meet with in our fellow-creatures?

"We all," says 2 Cor 3:18, "who with unveiled faces contemplate the Lord's glory, are being transformed into his image with ever-increasing glory, which comes from the Lord, who is the Spirit." We are changed by looking at the glory of God in the face of Jesus Christ. It is this principle that Scougal is elaborating in the following paragraphs. As God's glory captures our hearts, rival desires fade into the background. We can put this into practice when temptations arise by matching some characteristic of Christ's nature or work to our temptation so that we remind ourselves how Christ is better than any short-term pleasure offered by sin. Or we can start with the truth as we read in the Scriptures or hear it preached. We can match this truth to the challenges we face so that our hearts are captured afresh at those points where they are vulnerable. A great way to do this is to pray through Scripture, turning a few verses at a time into praise, confession or requests.

Shall we dote on the sacred pieces of a rude and imperfect picture, and never be affected with the original beauty? This would be an unaccountable stupidity and blindness. Whatever we find lovely in a friend, or in a saint, ought not to engross, but to elevate our affections: we should conclude with ourselves, that if there be so much sweetness in a drop, there must be infinitely more in the fountain; if there be so much splendour in a ray, what must the sun be in its glory?

Nor can we pretend the remoteness of the object, as if God were at too great a distance for our converse or our love. "He is not far from every one of us; for in him we live, move, and have our being" (Acts 17:28). We cannot open our eyes, but we must behold some footsteps of his glory; and we cannot turn toward him, but we shall be sure to find his intent upon us, waiting as it were to catch a look, ready to entertain the most intimate fellowship and communion with us. Let us therefore endeavour to raise our minds to the clearest conceptions of the divine nature. Let us consider all that his works do declare, or his word does reveal him to us; and let us especially contemplate that visible representation of him which was made in our own nature by his Son, who was the "brightness of his glory, and the express image of his person," (Heb 1:3) and who appeared in the world to discover at once what God is, and what we ought to be. Let us represent him to our minds as we find him described in the gospel, and there we shall behold the perfections of the divine nature, though covered with the veil of human infirmities; and when we have framed to ourselves the clearest notion that we can of a Being infinite in power, in wisdom, and goodness, the Author and fountain of all perfections, let us fix the eyes of our souls upon it, that our eyes may affect our heart-- and while we are musing the fire will burn.

CONTEMPLATE GOD'S LOVE

Scougal switches from a consideration of the excellencies of God's nature to the kindness of his love. "Nothing is more powerful to engage our affection" than recognising the way God's grace bridges the vast gulf between the majesty of God and sin of his people.

Especially, if we add the consideration of God's favour and good-will towards us; nothing is more powerful to engage our affection, than to find that we are beloved. Expressions of kindness are always pleasing and acceptable to us, though the person should be otherwise mean and contemptible; but to have the love of one who is altogether lovely, to know that the glorious Majesty of heaven has any regard for us, how must it astonish and delight us, how must it overcome our spirits, and melt our hearts, and put our whole soul into a flame! Now, as the word of God is full of the expressions of his love towards men, so all his works do loudly proclaim it. He gave us our being, and, by preserving us in it, renews the donation every moment. He has placed us in a rich and well-furnished world, and liberally provided for all our necessities. He rains down blessings from heaven upon us, and causes the earth to bring forth our provision. He gives us our food and raiment, and while we are spending the productions of one year, he is preparing for us against another. He sweetens our lives with innumerable comforts, and gratifies every faculty with suitable objects. The eye of his providence is always upon us, and he watches for our safety when we are fast asleep, neither minding him nor ourselves.

But, lest we should think these testimonies of his kindness less considerable, because they are the easy issues of his omnipotent power, and do not put him to any trouble or pain, he has taken a more wonderful method to endear himself to us: he that testified his affection to us by suffering as well as by doing; and because he could not suffer in his own nature he assumed ours. The eternal Son of God did clothe himself with the infirmities of our flesh, and left the company of those innocent and blessed spirits who knew well how to love and adore him, that he might dwell among men, and wrestle with the obstinacy of that rebellious race, to reduce them to their allegiance and felicity, and then to offer himself up as a sacrifice and propitiation for them. I remember one of the poets has an ingenious fancy to express the passion wherewith he found himself overcome after a long resistance: that the god of love had shot all his golden arrows at him, but could never pierce his heart, till at length he put himself into the bow, and darted himself straight into his breast. Methinks this does some way adumbrate God's method of dealing with men. He had long contended with a stubborn world, and thrown down many a blessing upon them; and when all his other gifts could not prevail, he at last made a gift of himself, to testify his affection and engage theirs.

The account which we have of our Saviour's life in the gospel, does all along present us with the story of his love: all the pains that he took, and the troubles that he endured, were the wonderful effects and uncontrollable evidences of it. But, O that last, that dismal scene! Is it possible to remember it, and question his kindness, or deny him ours? Here, here it is, my dear friend, that we should fix our most serious and solemn thoughts, "that Christ may dwell in our hearts by faith; that we, being rooted and grounded in love, may be able to comprehend with all saints what is the breadth, and length, and depth, and height; and to know the love of Christ which passes knowledge, that we may be filled with all the fulness of God."

We ought also frequently to reflect on those particular tokens of favour and love, which God has bestowed on ourselves; how long he has borne with our follies and sins, and waited to be gracious to us – wrestling, as it were, with the stubbornness of our hearts, and essaying every method to reclaim us. We should keep a register in our minds of all the eminent blessings and deliverances we have met with, some whereof have been so conveyed, that we might clearly perceive they were not the issues of chance, but the gracious effects of the divine favour, and the signal returns of our prayers. Nor ought we to embitter the thoughts of these things with any harsh or unworthy suspicions, as if they were designed on purpose to enhance our guilt, and heighten our eternal damnation. No, no, my friend, God is love, and he has no pleasure in the ruin of his creatures. If they abuse his goodness, and turn his grace into wantonness, and thereby plunge themselves into the greater depth of guilt and misery, this is the effect of their obstinate wickedness, and not the design of those benefits which he bestows.

At the end of *The Life of God in the Soul of Man*, Scougal offers this wonderful final prayer:

And now, O most gracious God, Father and Fountain of mercy and goodness, who has blessed us with the knowledge of our happiness, and the way that leads unto it! Excite in our souls such ardent desires after the one, as may put us forth to the diligent prosecution of the other. Let us neither presume on our own strength, nor distrust thy divine assistance: but while we are doing our utmost endeavours, teach us still to depend on thee for success.

Open our eyes, O God, and teach us out of thy law. Bless us with an exact and tender sense of our duty, and a knowledge to discern perverse things.

O that our ways were directed to keep thy statutes, then shall we not be ashamed when we have respect unto all thy commandments. Possess our hearts with a generous and holy disdain of all those poor enjoyments which this world holds out to allure us, that they may never be able to inveigle our affections, or betray us to any sin: turn away our eyes from beholding vanity, and quicken thou us in thy law.

Fill our souls with such a deep sense, and full persuasion of those great truths which thou hast revealed in the gospel, as may influence and regulate our whole conversation; and that the life which we henceforth live in the flesh, we may live through faith in the Son of God.

O that the infinite perfections of thy blessed nature, and the astonishing expressions of thy goodness and love, may conquer and overpower our hearts, that they may be constantly rising toward thee in flames of devoutest affection, and enlarging themselves in sincere and cordial love towards all the world for thy sake; and that we may cleanse ourselves from all filthiness of flesh and spirit, perfecting holiness in thy fear, without which we can never hope to behold and enjoy thee.

Finally, O God! grant that the consideration of what thou art, and what we ourselves are, may both humble and lay us low before thee, and also stir up in us the strongest and most ardent aspiration towards thee. We desire to resign and give up ourselves to the conduct of thy Holy Spirit; lead us in thy truth, and teach us, for thou art the God of our salvation; guide us with thy counsel, and afterwards receive us unto glory, for the merits and intercession of thy blessed Son our Saviour. Amen.

Questions for further thought and discussion

1. *"When we reflect upon ourselves, let us consider that we are not a mere piece of organised matter, a curious and well-contrived engine; that there is more in us than flesh, and blood, and bones, even a divine spark, capable to know, and love, and enjoy our Maker"*

    Take a moment to reflect on that and to praise our Maker.

2. What else in that paragraph (page 32) does Scougal encourage us to consider? What biblical passages would help us to do that?

3. Scougal then describes the importance of reflecting on God's glory and *"his favour and good-will towards us."* What did you find most heart-warming here?

4. Why do you think this kind of meditation doesn't come easily to us? What factors are involved? Tim Chester mentions "mere intellectualism," what else might Scougal turn his attention to in the contemporary church? What might he say about your use of entertainment? Electronic devices? How might he encourage us to reform our church services?

Five ways that being 'in Christ' shapes our sanctification

There is a perverse streak in me which likes to tease my children in a particular way: when they ask about the meaning of a word, I will explain it using another word they don't understand. And when they ask what that word means I tell them it means what the first word means.

DAVID SHAW is the Editor of *Primer*. He is part-time Theological Adviser for FIEC and part-time lecturer in New Testament and Greek at Oak Hill Theological College, London. He's married to Jo and they have four children.

🐦 *@_david_shaw*

"Dad, what's a utensil?"

"Well, it's a kind of implement."

"What's an implement?"

"Ah, simple. It's a sort of utensil."

Yes, indeed. I'm a hoot.

In this article I want to explore how *union with Christ* helps us understand *sanctification*, but this is not a tease. It might seem like we are explaining one hard-to-understand idea by referring to another, but I'm convinced that setting them beside each other is actually incredibly helpful. As we explore what union with Christ means, we will find that it addresses all kinds of questions we often ask about sanctification: why is it so significant? How are we made holy? What does holiness actually look like? How holy can we expect to be in this life?

But before we dive in, two quick comments are worth making about method:

✳ Union with Christ is most often discussed in connection with Paul's letters. The language of being "in Christ" and many of Paul's images (being the body of Christ, clothing ourselves with Christ) all contribute to the theme. So we will focus our attention there, dipping into other parts of Scripture along the way.

✳ Union with Christ is quite a broad umbrella term, covering a number of different ideas, and people use it in different ways. For that reason we are going to explore it from different angles, under **five headings**, each time reflecting on how it shapes our understanding of sanctification.

The five terms are adapted and expanded from Constantine R. Campbell, *Paul and Union with Christ: An Exegetical and Theological Study* (Grand Rapids: Zondervan, 2012).

1. TRANSFORMATION

One of the oldest summaries of the work of Jesus captures this idea:

Irenaeus of Lyons is perhaps the first to express the idea in *Against Heresies* Book V, written around AD180.

He became what we are, in order that we might become as he is.

The goal of salvation is that we might become like God himself – united to him in that sense.

One of the reasons this term has become popular in recent theology is that it is a strong theme in Eastern Orthodox theology and so has an ecumenical appeal. For similar reasons, the New Testament scholar Michael Gorman has been writing about *theosis* (another word for deification). See e.g. Michael J. Gorman, *Inhabiting the Cruciform God: Kenosis, Justification, and Theosis in Paul's Narrative Soteriology* (Grand Rapids: Eerdmans, 2009). Wonderfully, that means you join in my childish games: if anyone asks you what deification means, just tell them it's basically the same as theosis!

This reality is itself described in various terms, the most debated of which is *deification* – the idea that we become like God. There is, of course, an important sense in which we do not become God; we always remain creatures, and God's attributes of omniscience and so on are not shared with us. And we always remain ourselves; there is no thought here of being absorbed into and lost in a divine consciousness. John Calvin met these kinds of ideas and spoke against them strongly:

> *There are fanatics who imagine that we cross over into God's nature so that His nature absorbs ours... [but] this kind of madness never occurred to the minds of the holy apostles.*

Commentary on Second Peter (Calvin's Commentaries; 22vols. Grand Rapids: Baker, 1984), 22:371.

And yet you will find deification language used, even by Calvin, for example, when he explains the phrase in 2 Pet 1:4 that through God's promises we "participate in the divine nature." *"The purpose of the gospel,"* he writes, *"is to make us sooner or later like God; indeed it is, so to speak a kind of deification."* So we are saved, not to be God, but to be *like* God. In Calvin's words, *"the image of God in holiness and righteousness is reborn in us on the condition of our sharing in eternal life and glory."*

ibid.

ibid.

In other passages it is clear that we become like God *as he is revealed in Jesus*. For example, in Rom 8:29, Paul says that God predestined us "to be conformed to the likeness of his Son." In 2 Cor 3:18 he makes it clear that this process has already begun. The glory of God is revealed in the face of Jesus Christ and we "are being transformed into the same image from glory to glory." Accordingly, Paul expresses his great goal in pastoral ministry to the Galatians as a hope "to see Christ formed in you" (4:19).

SIGNIFICANCE FOR SANCTIFICATION

It is a generalisation, but one based on some truth I think, that evangelicals are often clearer on what they have been saved *from* than what they have been saved *for*. We know (and have needed to defend the idea) that our sins deserved wrath and that the punishment they deserve has been borne by Jesus. But what's next? And how does sanctification fit in? Is it merely that we have been saved and so we now show that we're grateful by living differently? Although it is certainly true that God wants us to see that his gracious provision of atonement should profoundly shape how we live, that is not the whole story. Some of the clearest places to see this are in the promises of the new covenant. In Ezek 36 we read God's promise to his people:

In his book *Future Grace*, John Piper rightly criticises the 'debtor's ethic' – 'God's done something for you and so now you owe him' – but there is a sense in which those who know they have been forgiven much will forgive others (Luke 7:39-47), and the preciousness of the blood that was spilled should affect how we behave (1 Pet 1:18-19).

Ezek 36:25-27

I will sprinkle clean water on you, and you will be clean; I will cleanse you from all your impurities and from all your idols. I will give you a new heart and put a new spirit in you; I will remove from you your heart of stone and give you a heart of flesh. And I will put my Spirit in you and move you to follow my decrees and be careful to keep my laws.

That is, God will cleanse them *and* recreate them as new moral agents, able to love and obey him. Saved from impurity, for purity. Likewise, in Jer 31 we read God's promise that *"I will put my law in their minds and write it on their hearts."* These things will be possible, 31:34, "For I will forgive their wickedness and will remember their sins no more." That is very striking. The forgiveness of sins is not the sum of salvation, rather it is the prerequisite for a new way of living and relating to God. As Michael Allen says, summing up this point, *"A definitive dealing with sin occurs as pathway and ground of participatory and transformative enjoyment of the Trinity in the Spirit."*

Justification and the Gospel: Understanding the Contexts and Controversies (Grand Rapids: Baker Academic, 2013), 66.

2. UNION WITH CHRIST

We have just said that salvation consists of being forgiven our sins so that we can enjoy fellowship with God and be transformed into the image of his Son.

In that sense, union with Christ is the goal of our salvation. More often, however, theologians speak about union with Christ as the means by which we receive those blessings. Luther, for example, develops the biblical language about the marriage between Christ and his church and applies it to the life of every believer:

Who then can fully appreciate what this royal marriage means? Who can understand the riches of the glory of this grace? Here this rich and divine bridegroom Christ marries this poor, wicked harlot, redeems her from all her evil, and adorns her with all his goodness. Her sins cannot now destroy her, since they are laid upon Christ and swallowed up by him. And she has that righteousness in Christ, her husband, of which she may boast as of her own and which she can confidently display alongside her sins in the face of death and hell and say, 'If I have sinned, yet my Christ, in whom I believe, has not sinned, and all his is mine and all mine is his,' as the bride in the Song of Solomon says, 'My beloved is mine and I am his.'

In this instance, Luther is emphasising the way in which we are justified by this union with Christ. But Calvin especially would develop this to argue that when we are united to Christ by faith we receive a twofold blessing (sometimes called the *duplex gratia*):

Institutes, III.11.1. Notice here there is both definitive sanctification (we have been sanctified by the Spirit) and progressive sanctification (we are called to cultivate blamelessness and purity).

By partaking of him (i.e. Christ), we principally receive a double grace (duplex gratia), namely, that being reconciled to God through Christ's blamelessness, we may have in heaven instead of a Judge a gracious Father; and secondly, that sanctified by Christ's Spirit we may cultivate blamelessness and purity of life.

In different places in Calvin the two blessings go by different names. Here it is reconciliation and sanctification; sometimes it is reconciliation and newness of life; sometimes it is justification and sanctification, but they always mean more or less the same thing: our sins are forgiven *and* we have been made new.

SIGNIFICANCE FOR SANCTIFICATION

The fact that sanctification comes through our union with Christ is important in several ways. First, it underscores that this is a great *gift*. It is not the case that justification is God's work and sanctification is ours. They are his great twofold gift to us. Michael Allen again: *"Sanctification is a gift and an action from God upon and to us, and it cannot be reduced to an area of our self-formation or soul-care."* Second, it reminds us to keep these two blessings together. Sometimes people will try to play off the forensic, courtroom language of justification against the relational, warmer language of new life, but everything we have said so far pushes back against that. Calvin makes the point vividly:

Sanctification (Grand Rapids: Zondervan, 2017), 197.

III.16.1

> *Do we want to receive righteousness in Christ? We must first possess Christ. Now we cannot possess Christ without being participants in His sanctification, since He cannot be torn to pieces. Since, I say, the Lord Jesus never gives anyone the enjoyment of his benefits except in giving himself, he gives them both together and never one without the other.*

3. LOCATION

At the most basic level, to say that we are 'in Christ' is to describe *where* we are. Not literally of course, but metaphorically, we are in him. He is now the sphere of our existence: we were once 'in sin,' (Rom 6:1), 'in the flesh' (Rom 7:5), or 'in Adam' (1 Cor 15:22) and now we are 'in Christ Jesus' (2 Cor 5:17), or 'in the Lord' (Phil 1:14). That is how believers are frequently spoken of in the New Testament and it often involves a call to loyalty. A couple of examples might help illustrate that:

Rom 6:2-3

> *We are those who have died to sin; how can we remain in it any longer? Or don't you know that all of us who were baptised into Christ Jesus were baptised into his death?*

Paul is conceptualising sin here in spatial terms. As N.T. Wright so helpfully puts it: *"of course to remain in sin, in English and for that matter in Greek, will mean to go on committing sin, but Paul is interested here in where one **is** first and foremost; it is like saying 'shall we remain in France?' with the assumption that if one does one will continue to speak French."*

"Romans," in *Acts, Introduction to Epistolary Literature, Romans, 1 Corinthians*, New Interpreter's Bible 10 (Nashville: Abingdon, 2002), 537.

Paul's point, then, is that salvation has relocated us in ways that should transform our sense of identity and loyalty. We are to consider ourselves alive to God 'in Christ Jesus' (Rom 6:11).

That also comes out in Paul's letter to Philippi – a proud Roman colony where matters of citizenship and loyalty to Rome would have been cherished. But when Paul writes to the church there he speaks of their citizenship in heaven (Phil 3:20) and describes them quite pointedly as "God's holy people in Christ Jesus at Philippi" (Phil 1:1). The last thing he wants them to think of themselves as is Roman, or Philippian. Much more fundamentally, they are to think of themselves as being 'in Christ.'

SIGNIFICANCE FOR SANCTIFICATION

This way of thinking about ourselves has profound implications for our sanctification. We are all *somewhere*. Scripture teaches us to think of ourselves as those who are in Christ. Independence is not an option. There is simply either the realm of sin and death, or there is Christ. There is the kingdom of darkness, or the kingdom of the Son (Col 1:13).

John M. G. Barclay, *Paul and the Gift* (Grand Rapids: Eerdmans, 2015), 497.

There is no neutral zone in Paul's cosmos, no pocket of absolute freedom, no no-man's land between these two fronts. The gift of God in Jesus Christ has established not liberation from authority, but a new allegiance, a new responsibility, a new 'slavery' under the rule of grace.

4. INCORPORATION

The nature of that responsibility can largely be traced under this next heading. In a host of images, God teaches us to think of ourselves as incorporated into Christ.

We are, for example, his *body*. It is a picture of Christ's authority – he is the head, we are the body (Col 1:18, Eph 4:15). But it is also a picture of the need for increasing maturity in the life of the church (Eph 4:15-16).

We are the *bride* being prepared for our marriage to Christ. This speaks of his grace in taking the initiative and his tender care of us (Eph 5:27). The marriage image also clarifies the nature of our union with Christ – a wife doesn't lose her own identity in a marriage but enjoys a relationship that (ideally) combines intimacy with submission to a husband who expresses his authority in selfless care of his wife. Finally, the image captures the need for our devotion to Christ. If the story of the Old Testament people of God is largely a story of unfaithfulness or spiritual adultery, the call and promise of God is that in the new covenant we will be faithful to our husband Christ. We belong to him in order that we might bear fruit for God (Rom 7:5). In a similar way, Paul

WE ARE ALL SOMEWHERE. SCRIPTURE TEACHES US TO THINK OF OURSELVES AS THOSE WHO ARE IN CHRIST. INDEPENDENCE IS NOT AN OPTION.

sees the Corinthian church as a pure virgin promised to Christ, who is in danger of being seduced by false teachers (2 Cor 11:2-3).

We are also the *temple*, God's dwelling place by his Spirit. This is true of us corporately, as the church. In Christ,

Eph 2:21-22

> *...the whole building is joined together and rises to become a holy temple in the Lord. And in him you too are being built together to become a dwelling in which God lives by his Spirit.*

1 Cor 3:16-17,
emphasis added

> *Don't you know that you yourselves are God's temple and that God's Spirit dwells in your midst? If anyone destroys God's temple, God will destroy that person; for God's temple is sacred, and **you together are that temple**.*

As you can see in 1 Cor 3, gospel workers who seek to build on Paul's foundation (1 Cor 3:10) need to take care. They are never simply leading 'their' church. Rather, they are serving in God's temple, and he cares greatly for it.

This temple imagery also gets applied individually later in 1 Corinthians.

1 Cor 6:18-20

> *Flee from sexual immorality. All other sins a person commits are outside the body, but whoever sins sexually, sins against their own body. Do you not know that your bodies are temples of the Holy Spirit, who is in you, whom you have received from God? You are not your own; you were bought at a price. Therefore honour God with your bodies.*

SIGNIFICANCE FOR SANCTIFICATION

At an individual level, there are some striking lessons for us here.

First, remaining with 1 Cor 6 for a moment, notice that here Paul motivates us for holiness not only by referring to Jesus' past work ("bought at a price"), but also by our ongoing union with him by the Spirit. In the preceding verses this is pointedly applied to prostitution:

There is some debate about whether there is a reference to the Spirit in 1 Cor 6:18 – does Paul mean that whoever is united with the Lord is one with him in *the Holy Spirit*? Given the contrast between body and spirit, I think Paul is referring to the human spirit here. That said, the Holy Spirit is the one who unites us to Jesus, so his ministry is implied here, even if it isn't explicit.

1 Cor 6:16-17

> *Do you not know that he who unites himself with a prostitute is one with her in body? For it is said, "The two will become one flesh." But whoever is united with the Lord is one with him in spirit.*

Paul is arguing here from the lesser to the greater. To have sex with someone is to become one in *body*; Paul is saying that believers have become united to Christ in *spirit*, at an even deeper level.

The marriage imagery takes us further down this same road. To see ourselves as the bride of Christ speaks of amazing privileges and a call to fruitfulness. Our former way of life generated the fruit of shame and led to death, but now we have fruit leading to holiness and eternal life (Rom 6:20-22). In the old covenant, sinful desires aroused by the law bore fruit for death, but in the new covenant we have died to the law and now belong to another "in order that we might bear fruit for God" (Rom 7:4).

Where the NIV has "what benefit did you reap?" in Rom 6:21, the Greek text asks, "what fruit did you have?"

So then, our union with Christ has brought us into this relationship with him, but it has also brought us into relationship with one another as his people. The significance of that is easily missed. When I think about holiness, I so often think about it in individual terms – my own personal holiness before God – but these images of belonging to Christ's body and bride, to God's temple, encourage me to have a concern for our corporate holiness and to reflect on the ways in which my personal holiness is going to be expressed in how I treat and care for God's people. It is on the basis of that union, after all, that Jesus can speak of us feeding and clothing Christ when we provide for the least of his people. Care for Christ's people is not the only way to express our holiness, of course, but it is a big part of what holiness looks like, once we reckon with our incorporation into his body.

Likewise, the risen Jesus can accuse Saul of persecuting him, when Saul has been busy persecuting the church. Perhaps it was that encounter that first formed Paul's grasp of the union between Christ and his people. Subsequently, Paul then draws on the rich temple and marriage language from the OT to develop and deploy the theme in his letters.

Finally under this heading, we should return to that language of fruitfulness. The images we have looked at frame our responsibilities towards God and his people, but we have also begun to speak about the way in which our union with Christ provides us with power to live for him. Most clearly, it is there in the marriage imagery. As Paul sees it, we are now able to bear fruit for God because we are united to his Son. This is one of those places where Paul stands very close to John, for in chapter 15 of his Gospel we find Jesus' remarkable image of himself as the vine into which we have been grafted.

The vine image, like that of the temple and the marriage covenant between God and his people, is drawn from the Old Testament. It has a great deal to say about Christ's identity (he is the true Israel, in contrast to the unfruitful OT nation), but for our purposes, I want to focus on the way that this image of union with Christ speaks about the power this union provides.

Chiefly, Ps 80, Isa 5:1-7, 27:2-6, Jer 2:21, Ezek 15, 17, 19:10-14.

John 15:5 | *"I am the vine; you are the branches. If you remain in me and I in you, you will bear much fruit."*

For Calvin, this imagery proved, well, fruitful. One of his key terms for thinking about union with Christ was *engrafting*. We have been grafted into Christ in a remarkable way, which can be grasped once we understand some horticultural basics. When you graft or splice a vine onto an existing plant it will still grow and produce its own variety of fruit. But when we are grafted into Christ something different happens:

Commentary on Romans, on Rom 6:5.

In the grafting of trees the graft draws its nourishment from the root, but retains its own natural quality in the fruit which is eaten. In spiritual engrafting, however, we not only derive the strength and sap of the life which flows from Christ, but we also pass from our own nature into his.

That is, we do not produce the kind of fruit we naturally bear. Instead, we produce Jesus' kind of fruit. Or, in the language of Gal 5, we no longer perform the works of (our) flesh, but rather we bear **the fruit of the Spirit**.

The difference in language is significant in Gal 5. There are the *works* of the flesh, but the *fruit* of the Spirit, emphasising the Spirit's agency in producing love, joy, peace, etc. within us.

It should be clear by now that thinking about union with Christ as incorporation into Christ connects very closely to the theme of sanctification. It speaks of new relationships to which we must commit ourselves, but it also speaks of empowerment for holiness. The final question we need to consider is raised by that last point. Exactly how much power should we expect? How holy can we expect to be in this life?

To explore that, we come to the last of our headings: *participation*.

5. PARTICIPATION

The text Calvin was just commenting on was Rom 6:5: "*if we have been united with him in a death like his, we will certainly also be united with him in a resurrection like his.*"

Paul here is describing the way in which we have

been united with Jesus in his death, burial and resurrection – that is, we participate in those events. This is mysterious, to be sure, but Paul insists that it is a reality, and one which has wonderfully transformed our situation.

To begin with, we have *died with Christ*, or been crucified with him:

Rom 6:6
cf. Gal 2:20, 5:24, 6:14.

> *We know that our old self was crucified with him so that the body ruled by sin might be done away with, that we should no longer be slaves to sin.*

Paul will develop that thought in different directions in different places. In Galatians 2, it speaks of a brand new identity, where **our old self has died and Christ is all**. Here in Romans though it speaks of the way that sin's power has been broken in our lives. We are no longer slaves because our 'old self' has died – the self that lacked the power or will to resist sin.

I have been crucified with Christ and I no longer live, but Christ lives in me. (Gal 2:20)

And then Paul insists that we have also been raised with Jesus: *"Just as Christ was raised from the dead through the glory of the Father, we too may walk in newness of life."* We have a new self. Put another way, we are a new creation (2 Cor 5:17, Gal 6:15), experiencing the power of the new age through the Spirit.

My translation. cf. Eph 2:6, Col 3:1

Taken together, this death and this resurrection mean that Paul can exhort the church in Rome to consider themselves "dead to sin but alive to God in Christ Jesus." Crucially, this is not "try your best to act *as if* you were dead to sin," but "God *has* made you dead to sin so act in line with what he's done." As Paul will say later in 6:18, "You *have been* set free from sin and have become slaves to righteousness."

SIGNIFICANCE FOR SANCTIFICATION

At this point, I've no doubt that some readers are concerned that this sounds a bit too triumphalistic. Can we really be saying that our union with Christ brings about such a radical change? Well, there's no getting away from the strength of some of Paul's statements here and I suspect that many of us, wary of overly-optimistic views of the Christian life, are tempted to

We don't have space to get into the debate around Romans 7 and whether the 'I' is describing the Christian experience, or that of a non-Christian. Increasingly and, to my mind, persuasively, it is argued that Rom 7 does not describe the Christian life, but rather the experience of someone under the law, finding that sin is aroused by the law, leaving the 'I' incapable of doing good (cf. Rom 7:5). Crucially though, that view by no means denies a very serious struggle in the Christian life. That struggle is described in Gal 5, and as I will discuss, in Rom 6 and 8. Given that those passages are less controversial than Rom 7, we will focus our attention there. If you want to read more on Romans 7, I would recommend *Perspectives on our Struggle with Sin: 3 Views on Romans 7*, ed. Terry L. Wilder (Nashville: B & H Publishing, 2011).

For a stimulating discussion of the Christian life in Rom 6-8 see John Barclay's *Paul and the Gift*, ch16. He expresses the paradox of the Christian life not so much in Lutheran terms as *simul iustus et peccator* ('at the same time righteous and a sinner'); rather, "the believer is here described as both mortal and eternally alive, *simul mortuus et vivens*. On the one hand doomed to death, in a body that is bound to mortality, believers are also and at the same time the site of an impossible new life, whose origin begins in the resurrection of Jesus and whose goal is their own future resurrection." *Paul and the Gift*, 502.

downplay them. That said, a number of observations about the context and content of Romans 6 will help us to develop the pastoral implications of Paul's argument.

First, Paul is writing to a church he wants to see enthused about the gospel and its power for salvation. Throughout the book so far he has wanted to accent the sufficiency of the gospel of Christ. Christ, not the law, can justify (Rom 1-4); and it is in Christ, not the law, where we find the power to put sin to death and a secure promise of eternal glory (Rom 5-8). So Paul has a rhetorical reason for accenting (although certainly not exaggerating) the power at work in those who believe. In a different setting (Corinth, say) he will accent the opposite danger of getting ahead of ourselves. Significantly, this means that when we try to communicate the doctrine of sanctification we need enough self-knowledge to know where we are tempted to place the emphasis, and enough knowledge of our audience to know where they need the emphasis to fall.

Second, in Romans 6, Paul still makes it very clear that there is a significant ongoing struggle. We may have been set free from sin, but we still find ourselves battling against what Paul calls the 'mortal body.' It is there that we must not let sin reign (6:12); and it is to this mortal body that God will one day give life, when it is physically raised (8:11). This means that we live between two resurrections: we participate in a past resurrection, united to Christ, through which we are brought to new spiritual life, to new birth, born again of the Spirit; and we await a *future* resurrection when we will be physically raised, free from the presence of sin.

That creates a striking tension in the Christian life: we are alive in Christ, but still live in the mortal body. Its desires are still evil and need putting to death (8:13). The *flesh*, Paul's rich term for human hostility to God, self-reliance, and the source of our sinful desires, is still a strong force to be resisted even though Paul can also say that we have crucified it (Gal 5:24) and that we no longer live in it (Rom 7:5-6, 8:9).

Third, there is the very fact that Paul needs to introduce imperative verbs; *commands*. As soon as he has described what God has done by uniting us to Jesus he starts telling us that we need to think and act in light of it. We need to consider ourselves dead to sin (6:11, the first imperative in the letter) and then we need to resist obeying the voice of our old master, sin. We need reminding of the fruit of that old way of life (shame and death). We need to be reminded that giving in to the flesh is to collaborate with everything that is deathly (8:6, 8:13), and hostile to God (8:7).

These last two points especially should make us very wary of neglecting watchfulness and self-control. The struggle against the desires of the mortal body and the flesh will characterise life until the resurrection. And yet, the truth of our participation in Jesus' death and resurrection means that we are able to walk in newness of life.

CONCLUSION

As we said at the beginning, union with Christ can refer to many different things. Having explored the theme under the headings of Transformation, Union, Location, Incorporation and Participation, we have seen that it expresses the goal of sanctification (transformed into the image of Christ) and the means (we are sanctified through our union with Christ). Paul helps us to grasp the implications for us (we are located in Christ, called to be loyal to him and incorporated within his body, belonging now to him and all his people). Finally, Paul's emphasis on our participation in Christ's death and resurrection gives a vital perspective on what our expectations of sanctification ought to be in this life. Our old self has died, and we have been raised with Christ to an empowered and yet paradoxical existence: alive to God in mortal bodies. Raised to new life and awaiting the resurrection to come.

Questions for further thought and discussion

1. David promised that thinking about union with Christ would help answer these questions about sanctification:

   Why is it so significant? How are we made holy? What does holiness actually look like? How holy can we expect to be in this life?

   Did he keep that promise? What answers did you find?

2. How do the promises of the new covenant help us to relate sanctification to forgiveness of sins and justification?

3. How does union with Christ shape the corporate life of the church? How could church life better reflect that?

True holiness, we surely ought to remember, does not consist merely of inward sensations and impressions.

It is much more than tears, and sighs, and bodily excitement, and a quickened pulse, and a passionate feeling of attachment to our own favourite preachers and our own religious party, and a readiness to quarrel with everyone who does not agree with us.

It is something of "the image of Christ," which can be seen and observed by others in our private life, and habits, and character, and doings.

J.C. RYLE, HOLINESS

The Scalpel of the Spirit

Sanctification and the means of grace in the life of the church

*H*oliness is the great distinctive of the church. God planned to make her holy from before the foundation of the world (Eph 1:4). She has been saved from the world that she might be the holy people of the Holy God (1 Pet 1:15; 2:9). The holiness of God and his work in sanctifying his people is a core part of the Christian gospel.

MATTHEW ROBERTS is the minister of Trinity Church York, part of the International Presbyterian Church, where he has been since 2009. He currently chairs the Church Planting Committee of the IPC.

 *@MPWRoberts*

But how do we become holy? At least since the Puritans, the focus of British evangelical piety has been on an individual's spiritual disciplines: Bible study and prayer. As secular thinking came to dominate public discourse in the 20th century this has had to be supplemented by re-education in the Bible and Christian ways of thinking; we cannot be holy if we are not familiar with the word of the Holy God. Such things are obviously of immense value, and I do not want to oppose personal Bible study or private prayer in the least.

A rather different proposal for how Christian growth happens has been popularised recently by **James K.A. Smith**. Observing (rightly) that the Bible is at least as concerned with what we love as it is with what we think, and reacting against a perceived creeping rationalism in (especially) conservative churches, Smith proposes that we cannot change by educating our minds but only by training our desires via 'liturgical practices,' i.e. habits which both express and train our desires in certain directions. The result is that we must both avoid *secular* 'liturgical practices,' and embrace Christian ones. Liturgical practices designed to foster love for God are central to Christian formation, holiness (presumably) included.

See his three related volumes published by Baker Academic: *Desiring the Kingdom* (2009), *Imagining the Kingdom* (2013), and *Awaiting the King* (2017); cf. also *You Are What You Love: The Spiritual Power of Habit* (Grand Rapids: Brazos Press, 2016).

I want to argue that both of these approaches, while they have great strengths, have a great shared weakness. For they both omit something which for many of the Reformers, and for many theologians in the Reformed tradition, is central. It is this: Sanctification, along with all of salvation, is always a work of the Spirit; and the Spirit has chosen to do his work principally through the *means of grace* he has commanded us to use. And these means of grace constitute for us the right worship of the living God in the assembly of the saints: principally the word of God and the sacraments, accompanied by the prayers of the church. Thus the gathered worship of the church, far from being an event of our own design for the sake of our own edification of either head or heart, is an instrument designed and used by God to summon and save us, feed our faith, and sanctify us for his service.

Sanctification is a Work of the Holy Spirit

"Sanctify them in the truth," prayed our Lord Jesus for his followers. In so doing he made abundantly clear that sanctification is a work of God in us. *"Be holy because I, the LORD your God, am holy"* (Lev 19:2) is for New Testament saints not only a command but a promise. God will write his law on the hearts of his people by his Spirit (Jer 31:33; Ezek 36:26-27).

That it is God who sanctifies is a vital truth, for here lies an inescapable distinction between true and false religion. The book of Galatians can be seen as largely turning on the question of whether we sanctify ourselves that God may justify us (as the Judaizers maintained) or whether it is God who both justifies and sanctifies by his Holy Spirit by faith. The active work of the Holy Spirit in producing the fruit of holiness forms perhaps the pinnacle of the book in 5:16-26.

This distinction between the true gospel and *"a different gospel – which is really no gospel at all"* (Gal 1:6-7) was at the heart of the Pelagian controversy of the 5th century, and equally (though this often went unnoticed because it was mixed in with a raft of other errors) stood between orthodoxy and Liberalism as it arose in the 19th century and grew in the 20th, and still does to this day. Christ came to save sinners from the guilt and the power of sin.

Herman Bavinck sums this up in typical style:

Reformed Dogmatics 4:232.

> *Since the redemption that God grants and works out in Christ is meant to accomplish complete deliverance from sin and all its consequences, it includes sanctification and glorification from the very beginning, along with justification.*

The Spirit Uses Means

Indeed, one might want to observe that to found and run a national conference with the central aim of teaching this passive view of sanctification, as the Keswick Convention was founded to be in 1875, is a rather remarkable case of the end being contradicted by the means. (It should be noted that this original purpose was abandoned long ago and has no connection to today's Keswick Convention).

Occasionally evangelicals have taken this doctrine as meaning that sanctification is a purely internal, unmediated miracle, and requires no activity by us to become a reality. Such was the 'Higher Life' or 'Keswick' theology of the late 19th century, which urged that all we need do to become holy was 'let go and let God'. One obvious problem with this position is that the moment one feels the need to persuade someone else of it, so that they can become holy too, one has of course become a 'means' of that person's sanctification. Of course, there are much more substantial biblical objections too: the frequent urging of Christians to pursue holiness actively being the most obvious.

In general, therefore, evangelicals have been happy with the expectation of the Spirit making use of various sorts of means in our sanctification. The very existence of a large body of Christian literature offering guidance in how to grow in grace, faith and discipleship in every area of life demonstrates this, for these are themselves 'means'. And of course evangelicals (at least until recently) have usually seen the word of God as central to all such means: we need the Bible if we are to become more holy. Yet, as I observed at the beginning, evangelicals have most often construed this work of the Spirit through scripture *individually*: it is in prayer, reading and meditating on Scripture, self-examination, repenting of and mortifying my sins that I expect to become more holy. And while fellowship with other believers has been highly valued along with this, this has been of the informal kind of iron-sharpening-iron, rather than connected in any particular way with corporate worship.

The Principal Means are the Public Means

In more classic Reformed thought, however, the Spirit's principal means are public, not private, being exercised by him in the gathered worship of the church. Indeed we can go further than that; this, in Reformed thought, is what Christian worship *is*. It is the gathering of the people of God by the command of God so that he might exercise his means of grace among them.

Consider Calvin's description of how Christian growth happens:

We see how God, who could in a moment perfect his own, nevertheless desires them to grow into manhood solely under the education of the church.

Calvin, *Institutes of the Christian Religion*, 4.1.5

Calvin was not being particularly distinctive here; the whole **Magisterial Reformation** strongly emphasised the public worship of the church in this way. This connection between the Spirit's work and the church

The Magisterial Reformation is so-called because it affirmed the authority of the civil magistrate and a stronger connection between church and state. This is contrast to the Radical Reformation which called for greater separation and further reforms of the church and its practice, including the Anabaptists who rejected infant baptism.

was not new to the Reformation, for it is embedded in the structure of the Ecumenical Creeds. Nor did it end with the Reformation. The Westminster confession stated the same a century later in 1647:

> *Unto this catholic visible Church Christ hath given the ministry, oracles, and ordinances of God, **for the gathering and perfecting of the saints**, in this life, to the end of the world: and doth by his own presence and Spirit, according to his promise, **make them effectual thereunto**.*

Westminster Confession of Faith 25.3., emphasis added.

In his treatise on the Holy Spirit, *Pneumatologia*, Owen says that the first way in which the Spirit 'excites the graces of faith and love unto frequent acts' is 'by his ordinances of worship, especially the preaching of the word.' *The Works of John Owen vol 15* (Edinburgh: Banner of Truth 1965), 389.

Although Owen does affirm this clearly, it impacts much less than might have been expected in his treatment of the Christian life in his other works. Thomas Watson affirms the doctrine in these words: "Growth is the end of the ordinances. Why does a man lay out cost on ground, manure and water it, but that it may grow? The sincere milk of the word is given, that we may grow thereby. 1 Peter 2:2. The table of the Lord is on purpose for our spiritual nourishment and increase of grace." Thomas Watson, in *A Body of Divinity (1692)* (Edinburgh: Banner of Truth 1983), 274. This is very much in line with the teaching of the Reformers and Westminster, yet it has little impact on the treatment of sanctification and growth in grace in the rest of the book.

However, the Savoy Declaration of 1658, which revised the Westminster Confession for the Congregational churches, omitted this paragraph. This was probably not because the divines who produced it disagreed with what it says about worship (John Owen, for one, affirmed the Westminster doctrine in his other works); more likely it was to avoid referring to the "catholic visible Church." Nevertheless, from the Savoy Declaration onward the significance of public worship as the principal means of grace does seem to fade from English Reformed and evangelical piety, even for those who affirm it. This is in contrast with Scottish, European and American Reformed theologians: for example Francis Turretin, James Bannerman, William G.T Shedd, Charles Hodge and Herman Bavinck, spread over two continents and three centuries, all retain its central place.

The Case for Public Means of Grace

What underlies the Reformed view that the Spirit works primarily through the means he has placed in the public worship of the church?

The most fundamental answer is the view, reflected in the Apostles' and Nicene Creeds, that the church and the ministry of the Spirit are profoundly linked in Scripture. The Spirit of God is the agent of both creation (Gen 1:2) and new creation (Rom 8:11), and the church, as the nucleus of the New Creation, is his especial work. Jesus baptises with the Spirit (Mark 1:8-10) to bring people into his body, the church (1 Cor 12:12-13). It is not too much to say that the sphere of operation of the Spirit in the new covenant is the church of Jesus Christ. Indeed, the work of the Holy Spirit is to make the church holy: to consecrate her for God's service, justifying her by the righteousness and sin-bearing death of Christ, and sanctifying her in ever-increasing holiness so that she is fit for the new creation.

But what is the church whom the Spirit sanctifies? She is the *assembly* or *gathering* of the people of God, which is the meaning of the words *ecclesia* in the New Testament and *qahal* in the Old. This is a rich Old Testament concept grounded in the "day of the assembly" at Mount Sinai (Deut 18:16), when Israel first assembled to serve God, who had called them out of slavery to himself. And she assembled so that God could come down to meet with her and so that she could serve him; this is paradigmatic of all the assemblies to worship found throughout the Old Testament, and we cannot read the word *ecclesia* in the New Testament without seeing it as grounded in this paradigm. Of course the church is still the church when she is not assembled, just as Israel was still Israel even when not assembled at Sinai, the tabernacle or the temple. Nevertheless, it is the assembling that defines her.

Therefore, if the sphere of operation of the Spirit is the church, the assembly of Christ, then one would certainly expect that he will particularly operate when she is, in fact, assembled. And if his particular mission is the justification, consecration and sanctification of the church, then it is when she is assembled for his service that we would particularly expect him to do this work. Jesus' words confirm this. *"For where two or three gather in my name, there am I with them."* (Matt 18:20). The evangelical tendency to assume that this is referring primarily to a few Christians getting together for some informal prayer or Bible study needs to be dismissed for the mistake it is. Jesus is speaking of the formal assembly of the church 'in his name', an assembly in which he says that by his authority sins will be bound and loosed on earth as they are in heaven, and in which prayers will be especially heard. It is in this assembly that he will be present. He is picking up on the Old Testament covenant language of God dwelling 'in the midst' of his people, a covenantal presence to bless them, in the manner prefigured by (and therefore in a manner even greater than) the way God was present with the assembly at Sinai, tabernacle and temple. Of course, since his resurrection, Jesus' presence is mediated by the Spirit. Therefore Jesus is saying that when his church is gathered the Spirit will be at work in the assembly of his people in a way not paralleled anywhere else.

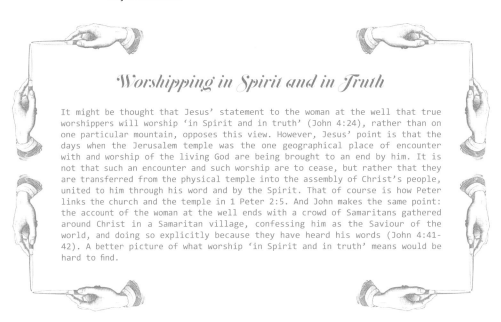

Worshipping in Spirit and in Truth

It might be thought that Jesus' statement to the woman at the well that true worshippers will worship 'in Spirit and in truth' (John 4:24), rather than on one particular mountain, opposes this view. However, Jesus' point is that the days when the Jerusalem temple was the one geographical place of encounter with and worship of the living God are being brought to an end by him. It is not that such an encounter and such worship are to cease, but rather that they are transferred from the physical temple into the assembly of Christ's people, united to him through his word and by the Spirit. That of course is how Peter links the church and the temple in 1 Peter 2:5. And John makes the same point: the account of the woman at the well ends with a crowd of Samaritans gathered around Christ in a Samaritan village, confessing him as the Saviour of the world, and doing so explicitly because they have heard his words (John 4:41-42). A better picture of what worship 'in Spirit and in truth' means would be hard to find.

The recent popularity of this view in English evangelical churches seems to stem from the article by I. Howard Marshall, 'How far did the early Christians worship God?', *Churchman 99.3* 1985. Its most popular recent exposition is probably Vaughan Roberts, *True Worship* (Milton Keynes: Authentic Lifestyle, 2002), ch4.

In the light of this it has to be said that the (rather recent) evangelical tendency to conceive of the gatherings of the church as being more about encouraging each other than about encountering God, more horizontal than vertical, is decidedly at odds with a biblical view of the church and the work of the Spirit. It can only be supported by the kind of exegesis that studies New Testament words in isolation from their Old Testament background and ignores their deeper theological connections.

So how does the Spirit operate in the assembly of the saints? Scripture shows us that his principal means are the preached word of God and the sacraments.

The Preached Word of God

God's word has power to save. The word of God is the sword of the Spirit; Jesus' words have power to raise the dead (John 5:25). Nevertheless, the Reformed doctrine of the word as a means of grace is saying something more than this. While the self-authenticating power of the word of God is the same at all times, God has so ordained it that the Spirit chooses to use the public reading and preaching of the word of God to the assembly of the church as the normal means by which he does his work.

Now lest we think that this is somehow saying that God is limited in how he does his work, Calvin explains: *"For, although God's power is not bound to outward means, he has nonetheless bound us to this ordinary manner of teaching."*

Institutes 4.1.5

Calvin is speaking of the ministry of the word of God by his ordained pastor-teachers in the assembly of the church. Of course God may work in any way he chooses, but he has decided to tell us to *expect* him to work in no other way than this, and, more importantly, promised that when we receive this means from him he will use it in us for his glory.

Calvin's main scriptural grounds for this are Eph 4:10-13, where Christ's gift to the church of the four groups of word-ministers **establishes the public ministry of the word**. Even if Calvin's reading of 'works of ministry' in v12 as referring to the ministry of the pastor-teachers is open to question, he is surely right to understand Paul's point to be that the Spirit brings the church to maturity through the pastor-teachers and evangelists proclaiming to her the words of the apostles and prophets.

ibid.

This is the presumption of every Old Testament text on the power of God's word, for private copies of Scripture did not, of course, exist. All Old Testament Scripture was designed and intended for public reading, preaching and singing in the assembly of God's people. In the New Testament there is a clear connection between the *preaching* of the word and the Spirit working in power to accompany and apply that word (1 **Thess 1:5-6; 1 Cor 1:21-24; 2:4**). While the words of the preacher himself remain foolish and weak, God has promised that his Spirit will make the word effective for the purpose he intended it. Throughout the Bible, the preaching of God's word is a constitutive part of worship every time God's people assemble before him. It is principally in the assembly, when Christ has promised to be present, that the Spirit applies this means of his work. We do not know how; we do know, for he has promised it, that he will.

Doubtless Paul has in mind the preaching in the market-places as well as in the synagogues and then churches, and it would be wrong to limit such verses to preaching in church. Nevertheless, the assembly is the principal venue for such preaching, and the only context in which it is both regular and required by God.

Many Christians have moved away from conservative churches because of a desire for a greater experience of God's presence. This is tragic because listening to a sermon, despite the obvious weakness of the human speaker, is transformed by the Spirit into a direct encounter with our God. In the preached word it is our Lord who speaks to us. We are hearing the voice of our Bridegroom addressing us, speaking to us as his beloved bride. To listen to him is to open ourselves to the surgical transformation of our hearts by the work of the Spirit.

The Sacraments

Nowhere is the gap between today's church and the Reformation more stark than over the understanding and significance of the sacraments of Baptism and the Lord's Supper. Accordingly, some background on the understanding of the Reformers will help us.

Luther perceived that Rome had inverted the meaning of the Lord's Supper by imagining that we offer the body and blood of Christ up to God, seeking grace in return. Rejecting this, he held that the supper was Christ sharing himself with us, by grace, and we are to receive him by faith. The connection between the sign and the thing it signified he held to be a physical one: the bread and wine did really become the body and blood of Christ for those who believe.

Zwingli famously opposed this doctrine strongly as too close to Rome in imagining a physical change in the bread and the wine. He held that the bread and wine remain as they are, and simply function as memorials of Christ's death, to increase our faith. Nothing happens other than that we are powerfully reminded of the cross.

Luther was horrified by Zwingli's doctrine, perceiving that despite Zwingli's intention it turned the supper into something closer to Rome than Luther's: Something we do before God in the hope of obtaining a benefit, rather than something he does for us out of his mercy. Calvin, entering the debate a little later, held that both views were defective, while each one's criticism of the other was substantially valid. He proposed a view of the supper which became and remains to this day the mainstream view of Reformed churches, the present author included.

Calvin's view is found in *Institutes* 4.14.

Calvin saw that Zwingli was right that the physical transformation of the bread and wine into the actual body and blood of Christ was unscriptural and impossible. And yet he also saw that Zwingli was in some ways more wrong than Luther. For it is of the very nature of the gospel that all good things come from God, by his initiative, and are worked by his power. Christ commanded us to celebrate the supper because it is emphatically *the Spirit's* instrument, not ours. It is not something we do for ourselves. Zwingli's doctrine takes away from believers the feast of fellowship with himself that

Christ lays before us, and makes of the supper a mere post-it note reminder that we write to ourselves.

Yet Luther's belief that the grace which Christ gives us in the supper is mediated by his physical body could not be right. Calvin's position therefore was that Christ does indeed share himself with us in the supper. Through the supper the Spirit really does unite us to Christ, body and soul, as he is seated in heaven at God's right hand. Through the supper we really do receive from Christ, our head, all his benefits. But if we ask of the nature of this sacramental union between the sign and the thing signified, the only answer is that it is through the promise of God's word applied by the mysterious work of the Spirit when we receive that promise in faith.

The same is true of baptism in a Reformed perspective. It is not something we do to declare or strengthen our own faith; it is something Christ does for us by the Spirit. We do not and cannot understand how the Spirit uses the water of baptism any more than how he uses the bread and the wine. But we do know that he has promised to, and that if we receive baptism and the supper in faith in that promise, then he will. Indeed, Christian faith is nothing other than faith in the promises Christ made to us in our baptism.

This makes sense of the numerous occasions in Scripture where the sacraments are said to accomplish something, while not allowing that something to be accomplished apart from faith in the promises of God. **Baptism saves us, in the Supper we participate in Christ's body and blood;** not in any automatic or mechanical way, but by the real yet entirely mysterious work of the Spirit when we receive them in faith. These physical signs with a Spiritual promise attached, fitted to our nature as physical and spiritual beings, are a means the Holy Spirit has provided and commanded, that he may use them to drive the gospel into our hearts. He uses them to strengthen our faith, to fire our hearts with love for Christ, to arm us against temptation, to sanctify us as the people of the Holy God. We do not know how he uses these things to do such things for us. But we do know, by his promise, that if we believe that promise, he does.

Those alarmed at these statements should note that I am only using them in same way as the Apostles did: 1 Pet 3:21, 1 Cor 10:16. The misuse of such biblical phrases in a Roman Catholic theology of the sacraments (which would say the sacraments do something automatically, regardless of whether faith is present, a view known as *ex opera operato* – 'by the work worked') does not preclude the right use of them nor justify ignoring them.

Prayer

In most Reformed treatments of the means of grace, prayer is not included as a separate means. This may seem a little odd, because it seems to be obvious that it is. Jesus' critical statement about when two or three are gathered in his name has particular reference to prayer: when two of his people agree about something they ask, it will be done for them by his Father in heaven (Matthew 18:19). Here then is a clear statement that God does respond particularly to prayers offered in **the assembly of the saints.**

The reason it is often not considered a separate means of grace is that it is probably better to say that prayer is a means by which we receive the other

Of course private prayer is a Christian duty, as urged by our Lord himself, so this is not in any way to reduce the imperative for us to pray on our own with the door closed (Matt 6:6).

means of grace. All prayer is a response to the word of God, for all prayer is offered to God as the expression of repentance and faith. In prayer we lay our needs before him and ask him to do for us what he has already promised in his word he will do. In Calvin's memorable phrase *"we dig up by prayer the treasures that were pointed out by the Lord's gospel, and which our faith has gazed upon"*; or, inverting the vertical metaphor, *"It is, therefore, by the benefit of prayer that we reach those riches which are laid up for us with the Heavenly Father. "*

Both quotes from *Institutes* 3.20.2

Therefore it is not really possible to separate prayer out as a distinct means of grace from the word and the sacraments, although there is clearly no harm in calling it such.

The Means of Grace and Congregational Worship

Let us draw out some implications for the lives of ourselves and our churches.

1. We need to stop seeing our church gatherings as merely 'meetings' of believers. Many of us (the present author included) have in the past dropped the word 'service' for our gatherings because we forgot (or never knew) what it refers to. But 'service' of God is exactly what we have gathered for: to put ourselves **at the service of the living God**, that he may meet with us by his Spirit and do his work among us by his word and sacraments received with prayer, as he has promised. We have not met primarily to edify one another but primarily to be edified and sanctified by God as we worship him together.

Note that the prototypical assembly at Sinai is referred to in advance by the LORD as the people 'serving' him (Exodus 3:12; 4:23; 7:16; 8:1,20; 9:1,13; 10:3,26).

2. For the same reason, we need to re-centre our Christian lives on the church's assembling to worship. The assembly of the church is not a filling station were we are equipped and fuelled to go and do the real business of Christianity elsewhere. It is the centre and focus of all of our lives, the place to which salvation by faith calls us, the place where our Holy God meets with us and fashions us into his holy images.

3. This puts corporate worship at the centre of pastoral care for the saints. Ministers who want to see their flock grow in repentance, faith and holiness, who want to encourage the discouraged, strengthen the weak and humble the proud, need to do all they can to urge them all to be present and to participate rightly in the assembled worship of God. This is not all that they need (far from it), but it is indispensable.

4. We need to realise that the church's main weekly assembly to worship God is, while far from sufficient for a church's evangelism, nevertheless a central part of it. Sanctification is part of conversion, as the Spirit turns the heart from unbelief to faith in Christ; and so if God particularly sanctifies through the means of grace in assembled worship then we should be keen to invite unbelievers to come along to our services to hear the word of God, and witness (though of course not join in with) the sacraments. This does not mean that we should dumb down our services to the level of someone who knows nothing of Christ, but rather that we should have confidence that Christ will work by the means he has given even in those who as yet have no faith. Of course God's word both saves some and hardens others, and both are (though in rather different senses) the work of the Spirit.

5. We must give careful consideration to the content of our services. It will be helpful here to return to the thesis advanced by James K.A. Smith. That thesis was that since human beings are shaped and defined more by what they love than by what they think, and since our liturgical practices shape what we love, often without us thinking about them, our liturgical practices of worship are far more formative for Christians than the doctrine we are taught.

There is a good deal of truth in Smith's analysis, both of the nature of humanity and the powerful influence of what he calls 'secular liturgies' (such as visiting a shopping mall) have upon us. The centrality of idolatry and covetousness to the nature of sin (Exodus 20; Colossians 3:5) says as much. It is also true that the Enlightenment operated with a deeply false view of humanity which thought of us as rational beings driven by logical thought alone. It is equally, and more sadly, true that this rationalist account of humanity has deeply infected the church, and most often the more conservative end of the church. Much fruitful thinking about our habits and worship will come from a careful appraisal of what he says.

Yet there are considerable problems with his approach as well. The first of these is that, though he makes some attempts to avoid it, he rejects a 'brain on a stick' anthropology (his phrase) only in favour of an equally unbiblical 'heart on a stick' (my phrase). For him, the mind is almost entirely relegated to **a subsidiary position.**

Smith acknowledges that there is two-way traffic between what we think and what we love, but he comes down decidedly on the side of the priority of our love expressed in habits; "the practices precede the understanding." (*Desiring the Kingdom*, 67 n53). While this may well be true in the individual experience of some Christians, it certainly is not true that our desires ultimately can't be articulated (51) or that belief does not include 'propositions that require assent' (*ibid.* 63). It is false to divorce the mind from the heart, but it is just as false to divorce the heart from the mind. Smith's move is in many ways a repetition of the oft-made shift from rationalism to romanticism.

Holiness is the great distinctive of the church

Salvation certainly involves the reordering of our loves, but it also involves their reintegration with **right thinking** (Romans 12:1-2).

Second, Smith's thesis sits very ill with the primacy of the word of God as the principal means by which God saves and sanctifies his covenant people. It is true that the souls of men, captive as they are to all sorts of false loves and lusts, will not of themselves respond to mere words. And yet it is equally true that God has so ordained it that it is his word – which addresses the heart through the mind – which he uses to achieve his purposes, both in creation and salvation. This is rather startlingly evidenced in Smith's statement that *"humans were religious well before they ever developed a doctrinal theology; and for most ordinary people, religious devotion is rarely a matter of theory."* This is positively muddled, and in an alarming way. This statement is true of idolatrous religion, but Christianity is emphatically not a question of people 'developing a doctrinal theology'; rather, it is by the preaching of the *doctrines* of God's word – the gospel facts of Christ's birth, life, death, resurrection, which are the subject matter of God's word – that idolatrous religious devotion is overcome and destroyed, and replaced with Christian religious devotion, shaped according to God's word. Of course the propositional truth of the gospel must be embedded in the worship of God which it commands and promises, or else we have not heard and understood it; but Smith's account entirely ignores that it is God's *word*, propositions and understanding, that call us to the right worship of the true God.

This links to a third problem with Smith's thesis. He ends up recommending warmly a considerable number of liturgical practices which have no foundation in God's word: lighting candles for prayer, *Tenebrae* **services**, giving 'a small clay ornament made by a local artist in the congregation' to baptismal candidates, among others. How Smith discerns the difference between what is an idolatrous liturgy and what is a healthy one is not easy to say. It seems to boil down to, if it's culturally acceptable to secular people, it's bad; if it's used by Christians somewhere, is strange to secular people, and can be construed as encouraging love for God, it's good. That may be unfair, but if there is a more fundamental distinction then it is not clear what it is.

The fact that his case is made in several carefully-argued books which (obviously) address the mind, rather than in some liturgical practice which captures our hearts, might be seen as a falsification of his thesis.

Desiring the Kingdom, 68.

Services traditionally held morning and evening in Easter Week.

Smith is aware of this view, of course, and it is the word and sacraments which are the focus of his attention, often very helpfully so. At times he seems to connect the Spirit's work in worship directly to those things to which God has attached a promise (e.g. *Imagining the Kingdom*, 152), which means that much of what he writes on worship can be read with great profit. But he declares himself 'not quite as worried about the mathematics regarding the number of sacraments' as the Reformed tradition. This apparently small concession has very serious consequences (as the Reformers would have told him). *Desiring the Kingdom* 149 n37.

In response to this, **one wishes that Smith had noted what we have argued here**: that since sanctification and all of salvation are the *Holy Spirit's* work (which in places he affirms), we as Christians are bound to the means the Spirit has commanded for us. The rather peculiar thing about Smith's analysis is that while he recognises and very helpfully illuminates Calvin's insight that the human heart loves to create and worship idols (which is why the secular world is full of liturgies expressing its idolatrous loves) he appears to forget that Calvin wrote in the context of a *church* that was inventing countless man-made ceremonies as part of supposedly *Christian* worship to express those idolatrous loves. And therefore Smith misses Calvin's central point: it is man-made ceremonies exercised in Christian worship that are a terrible danger to the church, just as much as any secular liturgies. In fact they are, in principle, the same thing. For what makes Christian worship *Christian* is that it is only those things which God has commanded for his worship which can be for us a means of grace. Christian worship is by command of God, not by the invention of man. It is a scalpel in the hands of the Spirit to work in us by grace, not a grappling hook designed by Christians to haul God's blessings down from heaven ourselves. And so it is in the humble hearing of God's word read and preached, despite the objections of the quasi-Romantics among us, and in the humble receiving of the sacraments, despite the objections of the quasi-Rationalists among us, that God is pleased to work.

This is what lies beneath the much-misunderstood 'regulative principle' of worship: the Reformed idea that worship should only consist of those elements which God has commanded us. If worship is a means in our hands for self-edification, then of course we may fashion those means as we like. But if it is a means in God's hand, his intended centre-point of fellowship between himself and his people, which in his word he has promised to use as his instrument of salvation, sanctification included, then of course it must be designed and mandated by him. Reformed theology has understood that this is what the second commandment is all about. To worship God in a manner he has not commanded is to expect him to act at our service, rather than to put ourselves at his. It is to assume he will act in ways he has not promised, rather than trust he will act in ways he has. It is to construe sanctification as fundamentally our work, not God's. Ultimately, it is to imagine we can fashion God in our image, rather than have him fashion us into his.

Conclusion

The Holy God has determined that he will make his people holy by the work of the Holy Spirit. And while he can and will use whatever means he chooses to do that, he has bound us to use the means of grace he has placed in the worship of the church with his promise to use them if we receive them in faith. Indeed, this is what Christian worship is: to put ourselves at the service of God, in prayerfully receiving and responding to his word and the sacraments, so that he in his grace may do his sanctifying work in us by the glorious, and mysterious, work of the Holy Spirit.

Questions for further thought and discussion

1. Reading over the first few sections carefully (up to and including *The Principal Means are the Public Means*), try to tease out: what does Matthew *disagree* with? What does he *agree* with but thinks we might have overemphasised? And what does he want to focus on?

2. *"God has so ordained it that the Spirit chooses to use the public reading and preaching of the word of God to the assembly of the church as the normal means by which he does his work."* How does Matthew argue that case? How widespread an idea is this in Scripture?

3. Matthew helpfully lays out the positions of Luther, Zwingli and Calvin on the Lord's Supper. Try to summarise what these are. Matthew's article defends and applies a Calvinist theology of the Lord's Supper. If that is not your view, is there still room to see the sacraments as a means by which God sanctifies us?

4. What does Matthew think James K.A. Smith has got right? What are his concerns and would you share them?

5. What might the significance of Matthew's list of implications be for your church life?

A SPACE FOR CHRIST TO FILL

JULIAN HARDYMAN has served as the Senior Pastor of Eden Baptist Church in Cambridge since 2002. He is the author of three books: *Maximum Life: All for the glory of God*, *Idols: God's battle for our hearts* and *The Joy of Service*.

🐦 @UncleJules

An interview about suffering and sanctification in the life of a pastor

Q1 – JULIAN, HOW WOULD YOU SUM UP THE THRUST OF THE BIBLICAL CONNECTION BETWEEN SUFFERING AND SANCTIFICATION?

The connection's pretty tight and you find it everywhere, in just about every New Testament writer as well as all over the Old Testament, for example, *"before I was afflicted, but now I obey your word"* (Ps 119:67). It is interesting that pastoral approaches to suffering changed greatly during the Reformation. In the pre-Reformation church suffering had been seen as punishment for some sins, necessary to shorten time in purgatory, while Reformed approaches encouraged believers to see suffering as a means to grow in faith and holiness. Both were very clear that suffering has a *telos*, a purpose, but very different ones!

There is much we do not understand about suffering but one thing is very clear in the Bible: suffering is not purposeless; rather it is intensely purposeful and a large part of that is our sanctification. Here are some supports for that claim:

1. Suffering is God's fatherly discipline. Not his punishment but his educational, training of us. Eventually this produces righteousness and peace (Heb 12:5-11).

2. Jesus himself only reached personal and spiritual maturity through suffering (Heb 5:8) and the same is true for us.

3. Suffering through voluntary daily self-denial is at the heart of the Christian life: we cannot follow Jesus or become like him without it (Luke 9:23-24). This means putting others first with the kind of love that costs us and brings us some sort of pain. It is all part of becoming a *theologian of the cross* as Luther puts it. Calvin sums it up: *"the more our hearts are gripped by the natural bitterness of the cross, the more they are filled with spiritual joy."*

See Carl Trueman's *Luther on the Christian Life* (Wheaton, Ill.: Crossway, 2015) and Gerhard Forde, *On Becoming a Theologian of the Cross: Reflections on Luther's Heidelberg Disputation, 1518* (Grand Rapids: Eerdmans, 1997).

Calvin, *Institutes of the Christian Religion*, 1541 edition (translated RS White, Edinburgh: Banner of Truth, 2014), 809.

4. Suffering is a test that produces perseverance and personal maturity with a kind of wise insight into life that cannot be achieved any other way (James 1:2-4). It *"burns the superficiality out of us"* and shows us what matters most.

Ray Ortlund, in conversation.

5. Suffering produces patience and teaches us endurance, deepening Christian character and enhancing our hope (Rom 5:3-4).

6. Suffering reveals to us how much we rely on ourselves, and forces us to rely more on God (2 Cor 1:9). Thus it breaks the sinful nature of self-reliance.

7. Suffering when we have sinned reveals to us that sin is bad for us and turns us back to God's path. It corrects us: an important thing! It curbs our natural instinct towards self-indulgence.

Calvin, *Institutes of the Christian Religion*, 809.

8. Suffering breaks our self-will because it forces on us things we do not want. So it makes us accept God's will both in Scripture and in the unfolding of providence.

9. Suffering helps us know Christ better as it takes us down our own version of the road Jesus walked and we find Him walking with us (Phil 3:10).

10. While suffering can isolate us, suffering can also force us to seek help from others and deepen our fellowship with them, if we are open to that (2 Cor 1:3-7).

11. Suffering now is the road to glory then (Rom 8:18).

12. Suffering puts on display – to ourselves and others – how weak we are in ourselves and how great God's grace is (2 Cor 12:7-10).

13. Suffering makes us long and groan for heaven more (Romans 8:22-24). This disentangles us from the over-attachment to the things of this world which we all have, the ultimately empty but enticing pleasures of this life.

14. Suffering disciplines us so that we are not condemned with the world (1 Cor 11:32) but eventually receive the crown of life (James 1:12).

To summarise: suffering has purpose: to make us more like Jesus; to make us trust and value him more; to produce maturity; and to get us safely to the joys of heaven.

Q2 – HOW MIGHT WE GET THIS LINK BETWEEN SUFFERING AND SANCTIFICATION WRONG?

First, Christians sometimes idealise suffering. Different traditions have done this in different ways but suffering is not inherently good, still less pleasant!

It is quite true that poverty, when considered in itself, is wretched. So too is exile, contempt, disgrace and prison. And death is the extreme calamity, but wherever we enjoy the breath of God's favour there is nothing in any of these things which does not contribute to our welfare and happiness.

Calvin, *Institutes of the Christian Religion*, 805.

That actually is the point. Calvin argues powerfully that we are not intended to live lives of simple joy, otherwise we would never learn patience. The *"bitterness which naturally gnaws at our hearts"* is essential because that is what we learn to resist and overcome in faith. Likewise we learn to rein in our natural outbursts.

Calvin, *Institutes of the Christian Religion*, 806.

Second, the training and purging effects of suffering are not automatic. Sadly, suffering can lead people to go backwards spiritually if they react angrily, bitterly or faithlessly to it – and one sees that in practice as people blame God or give up on him when they hit rough ground.

Third, we are not intended to respond with stoic indifference or a kind of otherworldly view that pain is illusory. Some Christians reject the idea that it is normal and right for Christians to groan, but that undermines the teaching of Romans 8 and the whole purpose of suffering: it is precisely through those groans that we can grow.

Q3 – HOW DOES SCRIPTURE HELP PASTORS SPECIFICALLY TO INTERPRET SUFFERING IN THEIR MINISTRY?

Suffering is in the pastor's job description: that is a major theme of 2 Corinthians. It has to be, because pastors (and other Christian workers) are to preach the good news of a crucified Saviour and live a life united to a crucified Master. For Paul this meant a near-death experience which gave him a significant step forward in relying on himself less and God more – combined with enhanced confidence in the working of Christ's resurrection power in his life (2 Cor 1:8-9). In turn the same deep agonies opened him up to Christ's comfort and made him more empathetic in responses to others in trouble (2:3-5). Hence Paul interpreted his suffering as given by God to make him a better pastor (1:6-7).

Pastors can and should interpret their suffering as making them better pastors for their churches. Pastors who haven't suffered much haven't as much to offer their people. Paul uses powerful images to sum up those in Christian ministry. "Jars of clay" (4: 7) is one that needs no explanation as the picture of fragile containers with very special contents (the 'treasure' of the gospel). So he can talk of rejoicing about his "thorn in the flesh" (probably a persistent and painful physical problem that he hated), because as he preached Christ with all the thorn's weakening effects very obvious, the gospel of a crucified Lord and of free grace was being communicated through his life as well as his sermons. A.W. Tozer is credited with the line *"Never trust a pastor without a limp"* which may be overstating it a little but is along the right lines. As I currently walk with a limp, I find that comforting.

Q4 – WHAT LESSONS HAS THE LORD TAUGHT YOU FROM YOUR OWN EXPERIENCE OF SUFFERING?

Objectively speaking, I don't think that my sufferings have been all that extreme, but my inner life has often been quite troubled by things that have happened to me – church difficulties in my early years in Cambridge, and family illness particularly – and that has often affected me a lot so that simple everyday life has been a big struggle at times.

The way I would sum up what I have learned is that every moment or pattern of suffering creates a space in which there can be more of Christ. It sounds a bit simplistic but it is my distillation of the biblical teaching. This principle – 'every loss creates a space for Christ to fill' – gives me an interpretative lens through which I can see my sufferings, minor and major, brief or extended. There's no pretending to know fully what God is doing but there is a definite seeking of purpose and opportunity in the nasty surprise or persistent disappointment. Christ becomes all the more real, precious and important when other props, joys and goals are taken away.

And I really have found him drawing nearer and making his grace more real, repeatedly and sweetly and with healing. Lying on my back in pain after spinal surgery in Autumn 2017, I found again and again either Christ drawing near to me by his Spirit, so that I simply had to be open to realise his presence, or that out of my emptiness I would reach out to him and find him again.

I guess I have also learned a bit about my own limitations; that the church seems to cope pretty well without me; that self-care is not a luxury but a duty; that regular and (sometimes) extended times of quiet, of reflection and of prayer are integral to my wellbeing and to my duty as a minister; that sin is not fun or helpful but grim and destructive; that my heart is still so blind and hard at times that I need a divine wrecking ball swinging to break it again; that God's patience is limitless and he loves me enough to let me experience surprising levels of pain so that I can know him better.

I found it very interesting (and quite encouraging I suppose) that after I had five months off with stress, depression and anxiety, people seemed to want to come and talk to me with similar problems. Since then my years of trying different ways of coping with continuing anxiety and variable morale also seem to have given me some things to share with others – chiefly that growing closer to Christ is most important (more important than symptomatic relief for example) and that any healing we experience is from him, even if he uses medication, talking treatments, self-help techniques, etc.

Q5 – HOW MUCH HAVE YOU MADE YOUR OWN SUFFERING VISIBLE OR PUBLIC TO THE CHURCH?

I have been pretty open about it, I think. When I had all that time off work in 2006, there was no point in pretending or covering it up with evasive platitudes so I wrote to the church myself and was happy for the elders to communicate how things were going themselves. Another time, after a sabbatical in which I had got very low and anxious, I wrote a report to the church in which I was open about the difficulties. I have often made references in sermons to my own suffering, though rarely while it was current. I have tended to avoid that because my experience of others sharing like that in sermons is that it distracts me from thinking about how the message was speaking to my own life because I have an empathetic response to them. For that reason, though God has brought my morale to a generally much better place now, I tend to refer back to my struggles with mental health in the hope that it will help others in some way.

Personal characteristics and pastoral situations will make a difference. Some people are more private than others and no one should be forced into disclosures with which you are uncomfortable. In an unsympathetic environment, personal disclosures may well be misunderstood or unhelpful.

In all of this I have been driven by one main thought – that Paul was very open about his struggles but in a carefully thought-out way, in order to benefit his readers. If he felt that he could share all that he does, especially in 2 Corinthians, it must have a pastoral point to it and be worth my imitation.

Once you start overcoming your inhibitions to disclose more, there are hazards! I have tried to work out whether I am trying to draw attention to myself, glamourise myself, or make a bid for sympathy. All of these are real dangers and clearly need purging.

Q6 – HOW WOULD YOU ENCOURAGE A YOUNGER PASTOR TO LEAD PEOPLE THROUGH SEASONS OF SUFFERING?

I remind myself often of this simple dictum: *walk towards the pain*. Suffering isolates people; not everyone in church, or even their closer friends, will find it easy to approach them or know what to say (though both of these things can and should be coached). But *pastors* must move towards people, making contact (phone, cards, email, messaging apps, etc.), asking how they are doing, listening at length to what they want to share, praying for them, arranging whatever support may be right, asking others to pray for them (with their permission of course). Pastors, who are generally used to doing lots of speaking, need to learn to listen (James 1:19), to be relaxed about long moments of silence when needed (which can be very healing) as well as to offer words of consolation from Scripture.

Sometimes a church *as a whole* goes through a particularly trying period. That happened to us at Eden when my predecessor left his family and ministry. It much more commonly occurs when a tragedy affects a church member or family. In these situations we need to give pastoral leadership to the church as a whole. That may mean simply acknowledgment ("this is a tough time for lots of us as we grieve for Jim"); it may mean adjustment in services: after friends of ours lost a newborn baby, the loss was announced in the morning service the following Sunday and after the service a group of folk joined them at the front to pray for them. If a church has been really rocked by a tragedy, the songs and hymns the next Sunday will want careful selection. Many of the psalms are laments: they can be sung very

...EVERY MOMENT OR PATTERN OF SUFFERING CREATES A SPACE IN WHICH THERE CAN BE MORE OF CHRIST.

a space for Christ to fill

helpfully, perhaps with a succinct word of pastoral introduction. We have sometimes had solos of lament-style songs. Many have found that helpful.

I guess in some special situations a pre-planned preaching programme may need adjustment so that a difficult situation can be directly addressed from the pulpit. In my experience, that has rarely been necessary but I have often found specific connections arising naturally between the text and the thing which is troubling folk.

There are two further errors to avoid: the first is just to quote biblical texts as if that settled the problem. The other is to do no more than listen and pray without really trying to bring the Bible and the person together.

Q7 – WHAT ARE YOUR FAVOURITE BOOKS OR RESOURCES ON SUFFERING FROM A BIBLICAL PERSPECTIVE?

There is no shortage of Christian books on suffering and many are first rate.

(Auto)biographical works are some of the most helpful for obvious reasons and there are many individual stories which help us enormously through the power of example.

➡ Jerry Sittser's *A Grace Disguised: How the Soul Grows through Loss* is one of the best as it combines the story of an appalling personal tragedy with careful theological thinking and an honest account the author's own bleak and bumpy journey of faith.

➡ Calvin is one of the best writers on suffering because he takes its interaction with our sanctification seriously and is more interested in holiness as the goal rather than happiness. His chapters on The Christian Life (*Institutes* III: 6-10) are probably the best material you can read on this and they are available as a book in their own right.

➡ There are many good things in Tim Keller's *Walking with God through Pain and Suffering*. In it, and in *The Reason for God*, he offers good answers to the so-called 'thorny' problem of suffering.

➡ Don Carson's *How Long O Lord* has stood the test of time really well: his biblical and theological expertise is very well deployed here.

➡ It has done me good to read books from different traditions. Among these the classic *Abandonment to the Divine Providence* (also, oddly, known as

The Sacrament of the Present Moment) by Pierre de Caussade insists on a response to suffering (moment by moment surrender to what God sends along in our lives) which is not much emphasised these days and thus a helpful corrective even if there are other things to say about suffering.

- A fascinating, detailed and deeply instructive historical monograph is *The Reformation of Suffering: Pastoral Theology and Lay Piety in Late Mediaeval and Early Modern Germany* by Ronald Rittgers. It did me so much good as a believer and a pastor.

- My own little FIEC Ministry Journeys book, *The Joy of Service*, focuses on self-denying service as the heart of ministry.

Questions for further thought and discussion

1. Under question 1, Julian lists 14 ways the Bible connects suffering and sanctification, but there are no Bible references for numbers 7 and 8. What would make good verses to back up those points?

2. As Paul "preached Christ" with all its weakening effects very obvious, the gospel of a crucified Lord and of free grace was being communicated through his life as well as his sermons." How do you think the gospel of grace and of a crucified Lord is communicated through our weakness?

3. In his answer to the question *What lessons has the Lord taught you from your own experience of suffering?* Julian begins a paragraph "I guess..." (top of p75). Read that paragraph again and consider what lessons the Lord has been teaching you. What from Julian's list can you relate to? What would you need to do to make some progress in learning those lessons?

4. In this article, Julian introduces three slogans:

   "Never trust a pastor without a limp"

   "Every loss creates a space for Christ to fill"

   "Walk towards the pain"

   Which is your favourite and why?

"

I WOULD SOONER BE HOLY THAN HAPPY

IF THE TWO THINGS COULD BE DIVORCED.

WERE IT POSSIBLE FOR A MAN

ALWAYS TO SORROW AND YET TO BE PURE,

I WOULD CHOOSE THE SORROW

IF I MIGHT WIN THE PURITY,

FOR TO BE FREE FROM THE POWER OF SIN,

TO BE MADE TO LOVE HOLINESS,

IS TRUE HAPPINESS.

C. H. Spurgeon, God's Grace to You